Mazes of the Serpent

An Anatomy of Horror Narrative

ROGER B. SALOMON

Cornell University Press

Ithaca and London

Copyright © 2002 by Cornell University

First published 2002 by Cornell University Press

Printed in the United States of America

Library of Congress Cataloging-in-Publication Data

Salomon, Roger B.
    Mazes of the serpent : an anatomy of horror narrative / by Roger B.
Salomon.
        p. cm.
Includes bibliographical references and index.
    ISBN 0-8014-4041-6 (cloth : alk. paper)
  1. Horror tales, American—History and criticism.   2. Horror tales,
English—History and criticism.   3. Narration (Rhetoric)   I. Title.
    PS374.H67 S36 2002
    813' .0873809—dc21   2002003064

Cornell University Press strives to use environmentally responsible
suppliers and materials to the fullest extent possible in the publishing
of its books. Such materials include vegetable-based, low-VOC inks
and acid-free papers that are recycled, totally chlorine-free, or partly
composed of nonwood fibers. For further information, visit our
website at www.cornellpress.cornell.edu.

Cloth printing   10 9 8 7 6 5 4 3 2 1

For Betty

In off the moors, down through the mist bands,
God-cursed Grendel came greedily loping.
The bane of the race of men roamed forth,
hunting for prey in the high hall.

        —*Beowulf* (trans. Seamus Heaney)

Contents

Acknowledgments

This book probably has some relevance to the terrorist acts of September 11, 2001, in New York City and Washington, but in fact it was written well before those events. In the 1970s at Case Western Reserve I began teaching a course called by the not-so-original name of American Gothic; I knew something about American literature, and I remembered that critics talked about its so-called Gothic tendencies. At least two curious problems very soon emerged: most students tried to avoid taking seriously what seemed to me (and, I assume, to the authors in question) very serious issues; and most mature literary critics were content simply to classify the genre by literary devices and cultural backgrounds. My own interests, however, got diverted; I wrote a book on the power of Quixotic illusion, before I began to think again of the nature of life without illusion. Out of such musings books sometimes come.

In any case, I am deeply grateful to the students, graduate and undergraduate, with whom I have shared ideas over the years. Special thanks go to three graduate students who helped me with research and with transcribing the text into computerized form: Ruth Rhodes, Rick Van Noy, and Kristin Bryant. My thanks go also to Suzanne Ferguson, then English Department chair, for warmly approving such an arrangement, and to John Bassett, at that time Dean of

Arts and Sciences, for offering me financial support that went even beyond my retirement. Finally, I am particularly appreciative and grateful for more recent help from a new colleague, Heather Meakin. She entered a good many revisions on disk for me and calmed my panic in the face of some important format changes.

In October 1992 I was invited by the late Darryl Baskin, Director of the Center for Mark Twain Studies at Ithaca College, to give a lecture at Quarry Farm, Twain's summer home and still a delightful setting. The talk gave me an opportunity to focus attention on certain more Gothic aspects of Twain's work, and some of the materials used then have found their way, much revised, into this book. In addition, I gratefully acknowledge the following publishers for permission to reprint copyrighted materials: Mark Taylor, "Descartes, Nietzsche and the Search for the Unsayable," *New York Times,* February 1, 1987, © *N.Y. Times,* 1987; Yale University Press for Charlotte Delbo, *Auschwitz and After,* © 1995; *The New York Review of Books* for Tim O'Brien, "Horror for Pleasure," April 22, 1993; Houghton Mifflin for O'Brien, *The Things They Carried;* © 1990 by Tim O'Brien; reprinted by permission of Houghton Mifflin Company; all rights reserved; Penguin Putnam for *Haunted: Tales of the Grotesque* by Joyce Carol Oates, © 1994 by The Ontario Review, Inc. and *Collector of Hearts* by Joyce Carol Oates, © 1998 by The Ontario Review, Inc.; both books are used by permission of Dutton, a division of Penguin Putnam Inc.; Penguin Putnam for *The Haunting of Hill House* by Shirley Jackson, © 1959 by Shirley Jackson, renewed, © 1987 by Laurence Hyman, Barry Hyman, Sarah Webster, Joanne Schnurer, used by permission of Viking Penguin, a division of Penguin Putnam Inc.; for *Beowulf,* translated by Seamus Heaney, © 2000 by Seamus Heaney: W. W. Norton & Company and Faber and Faber; Susan Brison, letter to the editor, *New York Times Magazine,* March 21, 1999; used by permission of Susan Brison.

Mazes of the Serpent

Introduction: Horror Explained (Away)

> All I entreat . . . is that you will abstain from forcing your own
> conclusions upon me. I want nothing explained away. I desire
> no arguments.
>
> —AMELIA EDWARDS, *The Phantom Coach*

> Driven by thirst, I eyed a fine icicle outside the window, within
> hand's reach. I opened the window and broke off the icicle but
> at once a large, heavy guard prowling outside brutally snatched
> it away from me. "Warum?" I asked him in my poor German.
> "Hier ist kein warum" (there is no why here), he replied, push-
> ing me aside with a shove.
>
> —PRIMO LEVI, *Survival in Auschwitz*

> This rage for explanation, for searching out the hidden mean-
> ing, is not limited to the early critics of *Frankenstein*. New
> modes of interpretation are in some ways no better.
>
> —GEORGE HAGGERTY, *Gothic Fiction/Gothic Form*

The narrator of a nineteenth-century ghost story pleads that we not
interrupt him as he tells us "the truth" about certain circumstances.
Primo Levi at Auschwitz quickly comes to understand the significance of the death camp: "everything is forbidden, not for hidden reasons, but because the camp has been created for that purpose" (25). A

I

critic of so-called Gothic reminds us, in an excellent phrase, that a
"rage for explanation" is endemic to critics of that form. There seems
to be a common theme here: that our human tendency in response to
horror is to rationalize it away; in fact, narratives of horror, whether
more recent accounts from actual battlefields and death camps or earlier stories in their various forms, are precisely those that deny the
possibility of such rationalization. At best, they may suggest some sort
of resolution ex cathedra—the opportune arrival of Beowulf, for example, to counter Grendel, "the bane of the races of men." The in-
credible or improbable (as Charles Maturin would call it) is reduced to
credibility by positivistic explanation; critics thus find themselves in a
position to deal with horror narration in a way that no one within its
narrative context is able to do.

In any case, in this book I eschew explanation, dealing rather with
what I consider a phenomenon of experience that cannot be explained (rationalized, schematized, ordered into a pattern), that in fact
deconstructs or otherwise mocks or casts in doubt all order or pat-
terns. Here I will describe the reality of chaos or nullity or some kind
of categorical negation. In effect, with horror we are dealing with a
material and metaphysical experience, with mystery, with that which
by its nature cannot be explained but can only be described as a phenomenon that impinges to a greater or lesser degree on the human
condition.

Nevertheless, all of this may sound like just another book on so-
called Gothic. My focus certainly does remain on literary texts that we
might call Gothic, though my intentions are to include these texts
within a larger aggregate of narrative. Perhaps, however, I need to deal
more fully with an obvious question: Why not put the word in the
title and deal directly with the issue? And, of course, a corollary
quickly follows: With so many excellent critical books on Gothic already on the market, why do we need another, whatever it may be
called? But it is precisely these questions that lead us to the heart of
the issue. The continuing proliferation of Gothic criticism has only

added to the lengthening catalog of various kinds of Gothic (beginning with lists of types of Gothic and Gothic conventions), these kinds now predicated on various sophisticated thematic explanations (feminist, psychoanalytic, political) of the significance of Gothic experience. The comments of David Punter, editor of *A Companion to the Gothic,* may be taken as representative of this kind of culturally contextualized explanation. His concern, he notes, is to show "that Gothic was, from its very inception, a form that related very closely to issues of national assertion and social organisation, and which even on occasion, could 'take the stage' in foregrounding social issues and informing social consciousness" (xi). Moreover, such explanations inevitably focus on certain texts and neglect others; in particular, the nineteenth-century ghost story is often underrepresented. Finally, a note of exhaustion intrudes, especially if we push our discussion into pop culture; almost in despair one contemporary critic, Judith Halberstam, notes that she does "not have any room . . . to catalogue the horror genre in any kind of comprehensive manner" (25).

But probably a third, even more important question lurks in the background: Why do I confidently elide more purely fictional narratives with those that clearly have a strong historical dimension? Again, the issue involves explanations, which always seem to miss or otherwise avoid the full implications of horror. In fact, horror can be empirical—an actual dimension of some physical reality, sometimes the most significant one—a physical as well as a metaphysical possibility, a human experience that may exist, on occasion, apart from any explicit narrative dimension. This is the point I emphasize as opposed to all those who deal with it as subjective experience or symbolic of something with a clear external referent. The crucial thing about the Holocaust is that it was a fact beyond mere imaginative perceptions, beyond nightmare as a kind of dream, beyond experience literally subjective or used primarily as metaphor of subjective experience or experience essentially responsive to the overthrow of some oppressive cultural pattern (e.g., patriarchy). Probably, I should add, beyond the possibilities of language itself. Years ago, in dealing with the horror story in its written and oral forms, Susan Stewart (following Tzvetan Todorov) noted that the function of language in such stories was largely to "unsettle" abstractions. In other words, even in its more verbal forms horror threatens "our hierarchies of relevance, our assumptions of the social, and our faith in the reliability of the self and its potential for apprehending the real" ("Epistemology of the Horror Story" 48). To be sure, we undoubtedly get some sort of gratification from horror stories—fascination and excitement, the imaginative experience of terror and loss, or perhaps merely relief and gratitude ("Thank God I'm not there"). Obviously there is some dimension of distancing in all art, whether we are talking about joy, horror, or any other human experience. Nevertheless, I suspect that readers and critics of horror have been more threatened by its implications than they may have realized, and therefore more intent on denying its irreparable irrationality.

In invoking the Holocaust, let me add that I am making no pretense of being a historian of this period or scholar of Holocaust narrative. Attempting to isolate horror narrative as a certain kind of writing about a certain kind of experience, however, I refer to Lawrence Langer's book *Holocaust Testimonies*. Among other things, it reminds us of the substantiality of memory affirmed by the act of witnessing. As Langer puts it: "At its frankest and most intimate moments, humiliated memory plunges into an erratic universe void of meaning, spiritually adrift, remote from empathetic understanding, bereft of value" (100). In other words, Langer is aware and makes clear that Holocaust reality has implications that go well beyond the immediate period of atrocities and certainly well beyond personal contexts, however terrible. He refers elsewhere to "a modernized or modernist view of verbal and moral possibilities and limitations that need not be restricted to Holocaust reality alone" (177). In one form or another, this idea is a commonplace about modernism. Daniel Fogel, for example, writing about the influence of Henry James on James Joyce and Virginia Woolf, comments on the "side of James that makes him, in many recent studies, a key transitional figure in the development of fiction from a metaphysics of presence to a metaphysics of absence" (*Covert Relations* 140–41). In short, with narratives of the various killing fields of history we must associate these more immediate fictions that constitute in the aggregate a true literature of death.

Amid various sophisticated discussions of negativity in literature, horror narrative remains relatively neglected—perhaps because of cultural vulgarization, perhaps because its forms seem to materialize the radical nonbeing that is its major theme. But then this is the paradox of such form: to articulate nothingness, the ubiquitous materiality of death, the fundamental horror of reality. Horror narrative subverts the very idea of form—it is, if you will, a dark parody of form, reminding us of what our various rhetorics seek to conceal. If modernism invokes the metaphysics of absence, a metaphysics operating on many complex levels, then Gothic is the earlier and most explicit genre in which absence intrudes on the presence of reality and destroys it. Absence becomes the categorical subject of discourse, becoming itself a total presence and subverting all alternatives. Even a palpable ghost is essentially a denial of living presence; presence as, in fact, absence—death. Likewise, the vampire subverts positive presence; love becomes bloodthirsty death, endless life, nothing more than the overwhelming and continual presence of death.

We take for granted today that texts resist final and definitive interpretation. At the same time, we are ceaselessly reminded that decompositions of whatever sort imply some prior act of composition, ordering, structuring. But in the context at least of horror narrative, any such reminder becomes virtually a mantra of hope and belief, a flicker of lingering humanism. Can we, in fact, deal with mysterious texts that paradoxically solve nothing at all? Literary criticism, in one way or another, remains an act of hope and explanation. Can we explain without explaining something away, that is, rationalizing whatever happens until its fundamental irrationality is finally denied, until it is brought once again under the control of some logical system? In any case, de-

scription and explanation (of sorts) remain the possibly quixotic in-
tention of the chapters that follow. What they offer is a typology of
horror narrative, not a book organized by the analysis of individual
texts, by careful attempts to separate reality from fiction, or by efforts
to put the experience of horror in some specific cultural context. "To
explain the inexplicable": Lawrence Langer notes this phrase from
Charlotte Delbo's *Days and Memory* (Introduction to Delbo, *Auschwitz
and After* xi), and I will return to it in due course. For now I borrow it
by way of identifying my own intentions.

I

Alternate Worlds

Gothicism must abide on a frontier—whether physical or psychical—and it is not necessarily European.
                    —DAVID MOGEN ET AL., *Frontier Gothic*

The land [Vietnam] was haunted. We were fighting forces that
did not obey the laws of twentieth-century science.
                    —TIM O'BRIEN, *The Things They Carried*

As the problematic influence of *place* will figure . . . in our narrative . . . I think it strategic for me to *digress,* as it were; and to
provide for the reader a brief summary of the history (both authentic and "legendary") of the Devil's Half-Acre. For, while to
some knowledgeable persons the very name of the place connotes lawlessness, and mystery, and, indeed, the demonic; in others, I am afraid, it strikes no familiar chord at all.
                    —JOYCE CAROL OATES, *Mysteries of Winterthurn*

Let us begin our quest for a typology of horror with a meditation on
the environment of ghosts. But can we take the issue seriously? It's a
joke, perhaps; or, as Joyce Carol Oates ironically suggests, "it strikes no
familiar chord at all" (158–59). For the modern rational mind at least,
ghosts are easy to dismiss: inhabitants of Disneyland funhouses and
low-budget Hollywood films or the staple model of children's cos-
tuming at Halloween. But Tim O'Brien's comment on GI lingo sug-

gests that "spooks" (or "getting spooked") may have a darker resonance: nothing less than the immediate and omnipresent experience of death. As he writes in the same passage describing the haunted landscape of Vietnam, "we called the enemy ghosts. 'Bad night,' we'd say, 'the ghosts are out.' To get spooked, in the lingo, meant not only to get scared but to get killed" (228–29). The title of Pat Barker's novel *The Ghost Road* aptly links the horrors of World War I with those of a precisely invoked Melanesian culture.

Such language contains a cautionary note. Are we, after all, so sure that we can understand and explain all human experience, that we can confidently label all of life's "normal" processes? In the foreword to Ernest Hopkins' edition of Ambrose Bierce's *Complete Short Stories,* Cathy Davidson comments acutely that "the ghost calls the quotidian into question, not vice versa" (3). Bierce himself apparently had no doubts on the question. Davidson quotes him as writing that "nothing is so improbable as what is true. It is the unexpected that occurs, but that is not saying enough; it is also the unlikely—one might almost say the impossible" (2). Lawrence Langer has noted concerning Holocaust experience that "the impossibility . . . lies not in the reality but in our difficulty perceiving it *as* reality" (40). In all experience, actual or more directly literary, that invokes "the impossible," ghosts and other monsters are inevitably the central figures of dreadful possibility.

In a long and compelling essay on the horror movie, Geoffrey O'Brien notes a curious quality of repetition, calling it "a genre that seems to define itself by constantly recapitulating everything it has been . . . we always seem to wind up where we started" ("Horror for Pleasure" 63). And he adds, by way of elaboration: "It is an eternal return to the site of a singular unmodulated shock: a spook mask popping out of darkness" (64). O'Brien's comments hold true for horror narrative in general, and we must now pursue them in the context of specific questions: Whence comes this "spook mask"? Can we be reasonably specific about what dimensions of reality it represents? Finally, what is its relation to (all we would like to consider as) our normative world?

THRESHOLDS

Horror narrative involves thresholds—a narrative in which two worlds, settings, environments impinge, where crossing (and the resulting experience of horror) is the basic action. Movement (at least in many explicitly fictional contexts) can be in either direction in these mirror worlds. That is, some spook invades our commonplace reality, or our apparently sane and rational self enters a categorically malign environment. The poignant voice of a female Holocaust survivor reminds us that this duality is not without its historical imperatives: "You have [she tells an interviewer] one vision of life and I have two. I—you know—I lived on two planets" (Langer, *Holocaust Testimonies* 53). The extraordinary European battlefield situation of World War I reminds us of another historical example. Within a mile or so of a fixed trench line the landscape was a deadly, barren wasteland. Yet behind the line, a sensuous, largely pastoral France continued to exist more or less normally, and across the Channel England remained as a reality often deeply colored by nostalgic memory. In any case, the invocation of two worlds is ubiquitous in horror narrative. The dual worlds of *Dracula* are obvious and well known: In his first journal entry, the narrator, Jonathan Harker, crossing the Danube, senses he is "leaving the West and entering the East"; he moves on into the Carpathian Mountains, "one of the wildest and least known portions of Europe," a trip involving a "horrible nightmare" journey of wolves, cold, darkness, and terror (11–23). Harker's host, Count Dracula, immediately draws the significant moral: "We are in Transylvania; and Transylvania is not England" (30). Of course, the Count himself, in due time, will make a return journey to sane, rational, scientific, nineteenth-century England.

Always in horror narrative this alternative space exists—"at the out-skirts of the world," as T. H. White puts it in his splendid short story "The Troll" (Sullivan, *Lost Souls* 284). Yet always such "outskirts" threaten to subsume all space; "horribly tangible," these worlds and their inhabitants quickly serve to "shake one's interest in mundane matters" (280). In this case, Lapland, the environment of White's mon-strous troll, intimates radically, indeed, categorically deconstructive powers: "It had no boundaries . . . [a] curiously indefinite region, suit-able to the indefinite things" (285). Certainly in American literature the frontier is conventionally the place of encounter with some terri-ble Other. As the epigraph from *Frontier Gothic* suggests (and the book itself copiously documents), critic after critic has pointed out that to cross the boundary in the United States between so-called civilization and wilderness is to move from a rational order in one form or an-other to perilous and irrational disorder. Moreover, at issue here is not some true Manichaeanism, some true equality of opposites. Rather, like a terrible disease or malignant growth (a key metaphor), horror intrudes, encompasses, overwhelms. In William Hope Hodgson's "Voice in the Night," a shipwrecked couple, in spite of their best ef-forts, finally incorporate and, in effect, become part of a vile "grey, lichenous fungus" that everywhere surrounds them (Child, *Dark Com-pany* 260–72). What here literally takes place is everywhere in horror narrative at least symbolically enacted.

This pattern—the delineation of two apparently alternative spaces, the violation of boundaries between them, the overwhelming power of the more negative and deconstructive environment—is widely, al-most universally shared by horror narratives, explicitly or inferentially. Apparent exceptions not only prove but, in fact, strongly reinforce the rule. In *Frankenstein,* for example, the obsessed experimenter (like so many after him) is passionately committed to a world of occult sci-ence, invokes this world, and then must live with the horror he has called up. His creation, in turn, can live, if at all, only in the waste spaces of Switzerland and the Arctic. Joyce Carol Oates, with her usual combination of scholarly insight and creative talent, quietly reminds us in her "Accursed Inhabitants of the House of Bly" of the mirror world of horror behind the apparent Eden of Henry James's *Turn of the Screw*. In Oates's version, Quint and Jessel are, in fact, buried in a "catacomb," a "damp, chill, lightless place with its smell of ancient stone and sweetly-sour decay . . . a corner, an abandoned storage area, in the cellar of the great ugly House of Bly." "*Crossing over,*" as Oates puts it, has brought them there, and, vampirelike, "by night . . . they are free to roam" (*Haunted* 255).

Usually horror narrative makes explicit (as *Dracula* does) its dual environments and the problematic space between them. Algernon Blackwood's important short story "The Willows" is a case in point. Again the Danube plays a prominent role, and Blackwood's opening description is worth quoting in full:

> After leaving Vienna, and long before you come to Buda-Pesth, the Danube enters a region of singular loneliness and desolation, where its waters spread away on all sides regardless of a main channel, and the country becomes a swamp for miles upon miles, covered by a vast sea of low willow bushes. On the big maps this deserted area is painted in a fluffy blue, growing fainter in colour as it leaves the banks, and across it may be seen in large straggling letters the word *Sümpfe,* meaning marshes.
>
> In high flood this great acreage of sand, shingle beds, and willow-grown islands is almost topped by the water, but in normal seasons the bushes bend and rustle in the free winds, showing their silver leaves to the sunshine in an ever-moving plain of bewildering beauty. These willows never attain to the dignity of trees; they have no rigid trunks; they remain humble bushes, with rounded tops and soft outline, swaying on slender stems that answer to the least pressure of the wind; supple as grasses, and so continually shifting that they somehow give the impression that the entire plain is moving and *alive.* (Child, *Dark Company* 152)

Loss of color, loss of fixed shapes and familiar forms, endless and inde-
terminate movement—all these qualities and more identify "a region
of singular loneliness and desolation." Later descriptions only reinforce
these initial details; we are told of the disappearance of "human habitation and civilization . . . the sense of remoteness from the world of
human kind, the utter isolation." It is, in fact, "a separate little kingdom
of wonder and magic" (154). But the wonders are awful, the magic is
black. If Blackwood's alternate nature has some relation to nineteenth-
century romanticism, it is more to Melville's world of fright than to
any version of a benevolent Transcendentalism. Into this "alien world,"
as the narrator calls it (159), come two campers in a canoe, and they
quickly become aware that "we are intruders." Alienation and an increasing feeling of horror go hand in hand, "the feeling of being utterly alone on an empty planet." They become aware of having crossed
some crucial boundary. One camper says to the other: "There are
things about us, I'm sure, that make for disorder, disintegration, destruction, *our* destruction. . . . We've strayed out of a single safe line
somewhere" (183).

Concerning this alternate world, Blackwood has few doubts; his
clarity of description in turn sheds light on the invocation of these
worlds by others. It is "a place unpolluted by men," that is, both inhu-
man and unhuman, "a 'beyond region' . . . another scheme of life, another revolution not parallel to the human." A "veil" separates this
place from our more familiar regions, a veil usually opaque but sometimes diaphanous, one that can occasionally be penetrated (or seen
through) in either direction (184). For human beings, Blackwood's
other world finally means death, but in "The Willows" not that of the
campers. They escape—barely.

Local social and political contexts naturally play a large role in shap-
ing the particular place and configuration of these alternate worlds
without limiting their final significance. Obviously, for the nineteenth
century the Danube beyond Vienna served as a symbol of the bound-

ary between the "civilized" West and some vague, largely unknown, and certainly "barbarous" East. Americans have always had the wilderness that lurked beyond the settlements. For certain recent writers such as Tim O'Brien and Peter Straub Vietnam was the spook-ridden place. For the early John Hawkes (*The Cannibal*), not to mention all those anguished voices that contribute to the body of oral and written Holocaust narrative, the Germany of World War II was more than adequate. An editor attempts to separate Ambrose Bierce's war stories ("the world of war") from those of horror ("the world of horror"), but in fact there is a seamless relation between the two. The place of war is both a literal reality and a convenient and obvious symbol of alternate space. In Bierce's aptly titled "Spook House," for example, travelers in need of shelter enter an old, isolated, half-ruined plantation house and instantly find themselves "in darkness and silence . . . as if they had suddenly been stricken blind and deaf." But this is only the beginning of horrors; the place turns out to be a kind of charnel house. Opening another door, the narrator finds that "the only objects within the blank stone walls of that room were human corpses" (*Complete Short Stories* 158).

I have already pointed out that science fiction also can generate these alternate worlds, but then, so can all those invocations of "paganism" in the nineteenth and twentieth centuries, from Blackwood and Arthur Machen to H. P. Lovecraft and others. For eighteenth-century Gothic writers some essentially "Catholic" locus or setting often served as the place of horror. Most of the well-known and often clumsy Gothic apparatus—the castles, convents, dungeons, underground passages, and so on—serve to mark off this alternate space. Charles Maturin is a case in point. In a metaphor that might refer to all such terrible dark worlds, Maturin describes monastic life as "like the wrong side of tapestry, where we see only uncouth threads, and the harsh outlines" (*Melmoth the Wanderer* 57). The moral and spiritual implications of life in such a place are categorically negative: "pain and inanity . . . the sufferings of hell and of annihilation," malignity, despair—all of this "abyss of darkness" (85–89). Of course in Maturin's massive novel, the convent is only one of many nihilistic spaces.

ATAVISM

In their introduction to a collection of short stories called *The New Gothic,* Bradford Morrow and Patrick McGrath note that "such chthonic, claustrophobic spaces" have been a staple of Gothic from its beginnings, and they note further that "each was a vivid analogue of the tomb and each provided a site of inversion." They also identify the temporal implications of such "sites" (or what I have been calling "alternate worlds") when they comment on the melding of elements in Poe's "Fall of the House of Usher": "The coalescence of all these elements sets in motion a process of regression, decay, a collapsing back" (xi–xiii). Morrow and MacGrath's comments probably shed some light on Peter Straub's curious description of a so-called body squad in Vietnam (those who picked up and packed in body bags the mangled and putrefying remains of GI's): "They were foul balls, neither psychopaths nor actual criminals . . . but people from whom something necessary and social had been removed either at birth or through circumstance." Physically Straub describes members of this one group as "unshaven, hairy . . . unclean, missing a crucial tooth or two" ("Kingdom of Heaven," ibid. 251).

The killing ground of horror narrative can be imagined as either a universal and ubiquitous mirror space, "the wrong side of tapestry," or perhaps a special space within our so-called normal world. In any case, horror narrative is based on this primary act of imagination, and imagination, particularly (though nor exclusively) in the context of Western culture since the Enlightenment (committed to political, scientific, even a benign religious "progress"), insists, in turn, on substantiality. As Joyce Carol Oates puts it, in a statement referring specifically to Lewis Carroll's *Alice* stories but obviously shedding a good deal of light on her own complex art: "What solace, if the memory retains the unspeakable, and the unspeakable can't be reduced to a dream?" (*Haunted* 307).

In one way or another horror narrative reminds us of the unspeakable, usually as something we have attempted to ignore, deny, or otherwise rationalize away. Time, which Western culture has attempted to make over into some benevolent icon, either has stopped, has turned back, or possibly does not even exist. In one of Oates's stories, "The White Cat" (obviously a critical play on Poe's short fiction), the cat's eyes are described as having at the center "those black, black irises like old-fashioned keyholes: slots opening into the Void" (*Haunted* 86). In attempting obsessively to slay the cat, the narrator is, in effect, attempting to destroy nature, that is, the world of nature or one that incorporates a natural dimension, one that at least hovers over and behind our all too human attempts at various kinds of order, control, beauty, and reason. Oates's characters attempt to deny or otherwise evade or avoid this always lurking, dark, passionate world, the world for her (as I have noted) of James's Quint and Jessel. The issue is not really neurosis or some political or social iniquity or romantic dimension of the self denied or repressed so much as simply the inevitable and (ultimately) unavoidable dimension of this dark world as a central aspect of human attempts to live. In "Martyrdom," to cite one final example from Oates's work, man and beast (in this case, a rat) alike go through a terrible and never-ending process of birth, mating, procreation, and death—a process that denies to time any possible redemptive dimension. As some appalled narrative voice says: *"And the horror of it washed over me suddenly: I cannot die, I am multiplied to infinity"* (*Haunted* 296; Oates's italics).

Insofar as Western culture has been committed for at least two hundred years to moral and physical "progress"—presumably the positive direction that empirical science, industrialism, and evolution must be taking—horror narrative seems to remind us that such progress is either seriously incomplete or possibly nonexistent, more comforting myth than measurable fact. In writing about the horror film, Geoffrey O'Brien notes that the malefic in such films is "primordial. It gives evidence of its proximity to the origin, the omphalos, by hovering around the scrolls, chants, bracelets, tiaras, and sacrificial altars of buried civilizations" ("Horror for Pleasure" 64). Of course, such atavism may have immediate and local referents. Another critic of horror narrative, Victor Sage, tellingly relates Bram Stoker to the "new" scientific theory of the later nineteenth century that related criminality to some kind of genetic failure: "The idea was born that the criminal was a 'throwback,' a 'ghost of the past' and 'the relic of a vanished race' " (*Horror Fiction* 180–81).

But atavism in horror narrative has wider implications and is, in one form or another, ubiquitous. The members of Peter Straub's body squad are not (as he makes clear) actually criminals, but they are nevertheless figures with "something necessary and socially removed." In the context of horror, at least, they are conventional figures, in the sense that literary conventions somehow reflect life experiences or that such experiences reinforce, reshape, and extend literary conventions. Like other dimensions of horror narrative, atavism moves us finally not to explanations but to mystery.

With Mary Shelley's *Frankenstein* we reenact a monstrous parody of the Garden of Eden—human beings beginning again with disastrous results. With Poe's *Narrative of Arthur Gordon Pym* we move from one appalling episode to another, toward a vague southern hemisphere of barbarous tribes and gnomic hieroglyphs toward finally a whiteout as all-encompassing as Melville's better-known treatment of the color white. Gerald Kennedy sums up a criticism of Poe's *Narrative* by noting that "we have come to understand the narrator's voyage as a series of interpretive crises which collectively suggest the unreadability of the signs constituted by nature and culture" (*Poe, Death* 145). More than almost anything else, atavism, in one form or another, serves to strip us of our metaphysical, moral, and cultural illusions and brings us, ourselves now naked, before the bare face of horror.

Such a confrontation precisely describes the action of Walter de la Mare's short story "A : B : O." Two antiquarian scientists (familiar types of nineteenth-century culture), following an old map, dig up a metal chest in the garden of one of them, and this chest holds, in fact, a "monstrous antiquity," an "aborted" travesty of a human being. The narrator reports: "I saw a flat malformed skull and meager arms and shoulders clad in coarse fawn hair. I saw a face thrown back a little, bearing hideous and ungodly resemblance to the human face" (Sullivan, *Lost Souls* 100). This "damnable thing" (100), this "vile symbol" (106)—these and similar terms are used everywhere—returns to animation and continues the kind of experience ("disease and death and springing up and hatred of life" [107]) that presumably it has always represented. Such an archaic figure, "springing up" in the pleasant back garden of an English house, makes nonsense of traditional forms of order and reduces both men to despair. The narrator's final response is categorical and typical of the human response to horror: "Science is slunk away shamefaced; religion is a withered flower" (106).

Everywhere in horror narrative the archaic holdover mocks the vulnerability of conventional signs or, paradoxically (insofar as these archaisms are themselves signs), suggests the potential if not actual failure of any sign system in the face of insoluble mystery. In her acute analysis of James's *Turn of the Screw*, Shoshana Felman notes that the story involves a "signifying chain" leading not to one meaning but to "the incessant *sliding* of signification" (*Writing and Madness* 215). While I differ finally from Felman concerning the implications of this "sliding," her point is well taken with regard to James's intentions in this story and to the endless attempts by critics to impose on it some single, clear, and rational meaning—critics, in this case, playing that well-known Western role variously called detective, scientist, doctor (especially psychiatrist), or perhaps some kind of analytic reporter.

At the very least, atavism in horror narrative challenges all our more benign assumptions about life and death. It serves to deny or reverse evolution, diverting us rather backward to the point of view of our "savage" ancestors, who allegedly dealt with the world outside the context of rational explanation. In Arthur Machen's "Red Hand" a narrative voice (obviously that of Machen himself) makes this position clear:

> There are sacraments of evil as well as of good about us, and we live and move to my belief in an unknown world, a place where there are caves and shadows and dwellers in twilight. It is possible that man may sometimes return on the track of evolution, and it is my belief that an awful lore is not yet dead. (*House of Souls* 489)

With Machen such sacraments (or their vestiges) simply deconstruct our conventional codes and lead us to a confrontation with horror itself in its continuing existence. "Who can limit the age of survival?" writes Machen in describing a murder by primitive flint knife in modern London, a murder that clearly marks the survival of some "troglodytic" figure, who leaves a "horrible old sign" on the wall as part of the murderous event. A skeptic in the story gropes for a "commonplace" and probable explanation and alerts us that he will have nothing to do with mystery: "I warn you I have done with mystery. We are to deal with facts now" (*House of Souls* 475–85). But he is overwhelmed by events.

In one fashion or another, horror narrative relentlessly attacks Western rational hopes, particularly those that involve our attempts to deny, postpone, or somehow overcome death. Atavistic appeals remind us of the naiveté of such ideas. In Ambrose Bierce's short story "A Watcher by the Dead" a secular skeptic, short of money, bets that he can sit up all night with a dead man. He asks himself confidently: "Shall I lose at once my bet, my honor, and my self-respect, perhaps my reason, because certain savage ancestors dwelling in caves and burrows conceived the monstrous notion that the dead walk by night?" (*Complete Short Stories* 77). The answer is yes; he loses everything, including his life.

Reinforced by the implications of much recent history, not to mention the recurrent challenge to comfortably unitary perspectives offered in the name of multiculturalism, horror narrative continues to offer a strong negative voice. Its categorical perspective is similar to that of Utopian fiction, but, of course, where one celebrates some benign future, the other reminds us of the relentless malignant power of the past. The house, presumably a center in society of beautiful forms and the longevity of family hopes, becomes, like Shirley Jackson's Hill House, dark, isolate, lonely, "vile . . . diseased," "a place of despair," a place "without concession to humanity . . . without kindness, never meant to be lived in, not a fit place for people or for love or for hope" (*Haunting of Hill House* 33–35). Forms affirm nothing except possibly the inability to move beyond infinite negation. Elsewhere this same house is described stylistically as "a masterpiece of architectural misdirection" (106). As the protagonist views it for the first time, her perspective is crucial and enduring: "The house had caught her with an atavistic turn in the pit of the stomach" (35).

Horror narrative endlessly takes this "atavistic turn." Let me offer a final example, a narrative that assaults Enlightenment attitudes directly and at great length in the name of an older, more generic appeal to darkness and mystery. One narrative voice in Peter Ackroyd's *Hawksmoor* is Nicholas Dyer, child of London slums, plague, and fire, who grows up to become Christopher Wren's assistant and the chief designer of his great churches—all the while despising Wren and everything he represents as a spokesman for the Royal Society and its "modern" scientific views. "They build Edifices which they call *Systems* by laying their Foundacions in the Air," notes Dyer at one point (101). At another he is even more categorical in his articulation of an "antient" point of view: "There is no Mathematicall Beauty or Geometrical Order Here—nothing but Mortality and Contagion on this Ordure Earth" (147). Dyer's twentieth-century counterpart (the word suggests little of Ackroyd's sense of their mirroring, shadowy, ghostly relationship) is the detective Hawksmoor, that is, someone who solves mysteries through rational processes; as he argues early on, "we live in a rational society" (158). But in this case Hawksmoor fails, and in failing moves close to Dyer's position of enduring mystery, darkness, and death. In the end, writes Ackroyd, "he saw nothing in front of him except darkness" (214). Again, so much for the redemptive power of time. As Dyer puts it: "Time is a vast Denful of Horrour, round about which a Serpent winds and in the winding bites itself by the Tail" (62).

MAZES OF THE SERPENT

"Who can speak of the mazes of the Serpent to those who are not lost in them?" asks Dyer at one point, and he goes on to describe sympathetically someone who "thought all the superficies of this terrestrial Globe was made of thin and transparent Glass, and that underneath there lay a Multitude of Serpents" (56). In *Hawksmoor* Ackroyd's serpent not only denies the secular and transcendent power of time but metaphorically (if not by some actual demonic presence) marks out the mazes that constitute those central places of horror, those "thin and transparent," scarcely veiled places that we cross into or that otherwise may intrude on our commonplace experience. Unfortunately, as I have noted, this issue involves more than a pattern of literary narrative. Tim O'Brien, for example, engages recent history by invoking the killing fields of Vietnam at night: "the fireflies and paddies, the moon, the midnight rustlings, the cool phosphorescent shimmer of evil" (*Things They Carried* 235). Few writers have captured better the peculiar but distinctive and categorical shimmer of horror. To be sure, O'Brien in this passage is negotiating the gap between history and fiction, but he reminds us at least that such places are ubiquitous in horror narrative, while not lacking historical referents. Let me simply review a few narrative descriptions of alternate worlds that are substantial and important enough but perhaps not well known. I will also avoid for the moment further direct commentary on the haunted house, the prototypal special environment of these antiworlds—the isolated, lonely special spot where the normal rules of our everyday reality do not operate. Obviously, in a wider sense, all the spaces that follow are haunted by forces totally destructive of human hopes and values.

Incarnations of Poe

Gerald Kennedy begins *Poe, Death, and the Life of Writing* with an acute comment on Henry James's "Altar of the Dead": "His altar becomes increasingly a tribute to death itself . . . he perceives his existence in terms of absence rather than presence. . . . His tale thus looks ahead to the twentieth century, to the metaphysical darkness defining the modern condition" (vii–viii). Kennedy's comment sheds a good deal of light on the development, popularity, and significance of horror narrative. If we assume that the loss of an authentic, positive, and vital transcendental dimension has been, in one way or another, an aspect of Western culture since at least the late eighteenth century, then we can more easily imagine horror narrative as moving into this near vacuum, even though, I must stress, the implications of horror threaten all systems of whatever time and place. In his great short story "The White People," Arthur Machen argues that "sorcery and sanctity . . . are the only realities," and he adds that "evil . . . is wholly positive—only it is on the wrong side" (*House of Souls* 113–15). The only alternative to some sort of transcendental commitment is what Machen calls elsewhere "the sane 'reality' of common and usual incidents and interests" (34), an option scorned by Machen and his characters, for better or for worse.

Usually for the worse. What Machen labels "sacraments of evil" are, by and large, the only sacraments that remain, and, paradoxically, they finally threaten the very idea of sacrament. In this case as in so many others, Mary Shelley's *Frankenstein* may be taken as a benchmark. Her self-conscious and sustained parody of Milton and the Garden of Eden story deconstructs that story to the point where any dimension of love, life, and order have been lost, and God—assuming he exists at all—now comes garbed only in the accoutrements of Frankenstein's amoral will and desire.

Machen's own creation story, "The Great God Pan," is, if possible, even more decreative than Shelley's. Again we have someone who describes himself with telling accuracy as a devotee of "transcendental medicine" (Child, *Dark Company* 104), and again, with an operation, he transports the victim (in this case a young woman) "beyond a veil" (104) into the alternate world of Pan, allegedly a world of spirit and vision, in fact a world categorically destructive to matter in any form available to us as human beings. Matter literally melts down in confrontation with the horror let loose. As with Poe, horror is miasmic; as with the flowers in the garden of Hawthorne's Rappaccini, the very smell is sinister. One of Machen's characters who enters a room that has seen the presence of horror describes the experience later: "It was as if I were inhaling at every breath some deadly fume, which seemed to penetrate to every nerve and bone and sinew of my body. I felt racked from head to foot, my eyes began to grow dim; it was like the entrance of death" (129). Here of course is the entire point; this alternate world, insofar as we may encounter it at all and survive, is one of dissolution and death.

"The Great God Pan" develops as a series of stories within stories, a Chinese box structure that Machen himself identifies (119). Machen's altered young woman, now an initiate of this terrible world beyond the veil, takes on various humanoid identities throughout the long narrative and everywhere destroys those who cross her path. "It is an old story," notes one of the more perceptive characters. The comment reminds us that horror narrative always tells an old story in deliberate response to the newer stories so significant to modern culture. His comment deserves quotation at some length:

> It is an old story, an old mystery played in our day, and in dim London streets instead of amidst the vineyards and the olive gardens. We know what happened to those who chanced to meet the Great God Pan, and those who are wise know that all symbols are symbols of something, not of nothing. It was, indeed, an exquisite symbol beneath which men long ago veiled their knowledge of the most awful, most secret forces which lie at the heart of all things; forces before which the souls of men must wither and die and blacken, as their bodies blacken under the electric current. Such forces cannot be named, cannot be spoken, cannot be imagined except under a veil and a symbol, a symbol to the most of us

appearing a quaint, poetic fancy, to some foolish tale. But you and I, at all events, have known something of the terror that may dwell in the secret place of life, manifested under human flesh; that which is without form taking to itself a form. (144)

The old stories, old mysteries, old sacraments, however important—indeed, of whatever central importance—can serve only to wither and blacken the souls of human beings. If horror offers an alternate sacrament, it can only negate meaning in any form we might be willing to acknowledge. The paradox of these alternate worlds finally is of a nullity expressed so vividly that it constitutes an authentic reality of its own. Horror narrative in whatever form affirms their existence, albeit our instincts, for obvious reasons, almost always lean toward hope, forgetfulness, even outright denial.

Lovecraft and Countermyth

Certainly the overwhelming power and authority of horror are continually affirmed by its exponents. As H. P. Lovecraft puts it in "The Horror at Red Hook," one of his better stories: "Age-old horror is a hydra with a thousand heads, and the cults of darkness are rooted in blasphemies deeper than the well of Democritus. The sound of the beast is omnipresent and triumphant" (*Tomb and Other Tales* 92). He emphasizes this shattering presence everywhere in his work; the protagonist of "Red Hook," for example, finally "delirious and hazy . . . gasping and shivering" (like Machen's "withering" figures), is "doubtful of his place in this or any world" (88). For the horror writer, the place or mysterious center of malignity must be vividly localized to be credible; at the same time, its manifestations (and the inferences drawn from these manifestations) must be potentially everywhere. The alternate worlds I have been describing constitute, in effect, the settings of a myth counter to the positive mythologies of later Western culture. In one way or another, horror narrative debunks some of our greatest stories, if only to rob them of their most cherished implications. Needless to say, much of the actual history of the twentieth and twenty-first centuries affirms such debunking.

Lovecraft's long short story "The Shadow Out of Time" is a case in point, one of the most substantial attempts (in his own work and in the context of other horror writers he admires, such as Poe and Arthur Machen) to spell out in detail the nature of the countermyth and to record its implications. He refers variously to Einstein and relativity (explicitly mentioned), the darker aspects of twentieth-century archaeology, and the psychology of dreams, not to mention what might better be called parapsychological issues such as the alleged continuity of consciousness over time in various forms and the nature of historical and cultural memory. His narrator/victim/witness (the roles significantly fuse together) is first an instructor of political economy, then a psychology professor, and finally, in effect, an archaeologist as he roams the badlands of western Australia (with a geologist, an ancient historian, and an anthropologist) in search of traces of the older civilization that ceaselessly echoes through his mind.

Lovecraft's countermyth comes complete with epic quester. Albeit unwillingly (his body had been taken over for five years by a terrible and mysterious double from some primordial past), the narrator journeys backward by nightmarish dreams to a place of hideous people and artifacts, then later more literally descends (or does he? "I was awake and dreaming at the same time," the narrator tells us [Child, *Dark Company* 314]) into a "doubtful abyss" in the Australian desert (317) toward the same place. Or we might say that Lovecraft (like Joyce Carol Oates, ever the scholar as well as the writer of horror) locates two places of horror in his story: the carefully described antiworld lurking somewhere in the past, yet lingering into the present and (by implication) future; but also the desert wasteland, more conventionally the habitation of horror. The latter he crosses over into, echoing the Danube boundary experience in *Dracula*: "We forded a branch of the De Grey and entered the realm of utter desolation"

(309). This last, he adds, is an "abominable, sterile terrain" (310), an appropriate place perhaps for the ancient markings he discovers, but one that makes their further implications almost redundant.

In any case, the thematic implications of these alternate spaces are clear enough. What the narrator calls his "pseudomemories" (310) separate him forever from the usual responses of our so-called normal world. Gone, for example, is any familiar and comfortable myth of time: "there was no such thing as time in its humanly accepted sense" (289). But, as usual, the implications of horror narrative are even more categorical. The avatars of the "Great Race" deny all human possibility; indeed, their actions constitute a relentless dark parody of such possibility. "It is not wholesome," observes the narrator, "to watch monstrous objects doing what one had known only human beings to do" (295). And he draws the obvious inference: "Nothing that I might dream, nothing that I might feel, could be of any actual significance" (294). "Blasphemy" (287)? Of course it is; Lovecraft makes the same concession that Melville made long before him. In fictions of horror alternate places can have only one blunt and unequivocal meaning: "Dark is life, dark, dark is death," as John Hawkes puts it in his own powerful novel of a modern ghost-ridden Germany, *The Cannibal* (155).

The Devil's Half-Acre

Joyce Carol Oates's novel *Mysteries of Winterthurn* consists of three interconnected stories in a landscape almost as elaborately laid out as the area around William Faulkner's Jefferson in Yoknapatawpha County. A small part of this landscape—not geographically its center, but morally its core—is the area Oates calls the Devil's Half-Acre. The very name, Oates suggests (in a passage I have earlier quoted as an epigraph), "connotes lawlessness, and mystery, and, indeed, the demonic" (157–58). This killing ground is associated with the recent terrible mutilation deaths of five young women, the earlier burial of four thousand Confederate prisoners (victims of the infamous prison on Sandusky Island), and, from colonial times, with malignancy and curse. By extension, Oates associates this terrible place with the lynching of one Isaac Rosenwald (an echo of the notorious Atlanta incident of 1913 involving Leo Frank), an association that by further extension includes the lynchings of African Americans and the Holocaust. The Ku Klux Klan–like perpetrators are pointedly called a "death squad" and described finally in a way that links them with all the emergent monsters of horror narrative: "not human faces, but ghost-countenances with naught but blunt shadowed holes for eyes—the demonic and the childlike here combined, in a way most perverse" (267).

I rehearse these incidents at some length to suggest the degree to which Oates, within a pastiche of late Victorian fiction, has assimilated the details of horror narrative to more contemporary concerns. Beyond even Lovecraft, she combines in her work the insights of a scholar with the skill of a major fiction writer. Such a combination allows her to explore the nature and significance of horror narrative, a genre for which obviously she has strong intellectual and emotional affinities.

In any case, Oates's protagonist, Xavier Kilgarvan (like Sherlock Holmes, Poe's Dupin, or Hawksmoor, a sleuth, a solver of mysteries), stumbles into the quicksand area of the Devil's Half-Acre and almost perishes. Almost too late, he discovers both the meaning and the severe limits of consciousness. Like Lovecraft's figures and other protagonists of horror, he comes in this terrible place to acknowledge the implications of the primordial:

By degrees, sinking, being sucked so relentlessly downward, to the febrific bowels of the earth, Xavier came to see that this was no merely local and finite space into which he plunged, but the *primordial, everlasting, boundaryless* Universe. Here, no World existed, for "existence" was but a phantom: this inchoate sprawling lapping sucking substance predated all extension in space, and all time,—and it scarcely needs be said, quite annihilated the very principle of Individuality. It had been given to him, to be *Xavier Kilgarvan* for naught but the duration of his heartbeat,—for the duration of his lungs' potency: and when these failed, as they soon must, he would pass over, unresisting, into the primordial Universe, where Time had yet to be born.

    This, then, is the greatest of Mysteries,—to which there is no solution: thus Xavier's ebbing consciousness bade him understand. (259)

Needless to say, Xavier does not solve any of the many mysteries in the book. He does somehow escape from the quicksand—his escape another mystery unsolved. We are, in short, dealing with what Clive Bloom has called "the literature of disjunction." In his explanation, "the dark passage that leads to the locked door becomes the paradigmatic scene, symbolic of the meeting of different worlds, the journey to the other side, the site of the inexplicable at horror's core" ("Horror Fiction" 165). We must now direct our attention more sharply to the inhabitants of this core.

2

Ghosts and Other Monsters

It had a misshapen body made of stiff felt that was mainly
shoulders and arms; the head was bald and domed, like an em-
bryo's; the nose was a snubbed little piece of cotton made pre-
hensile by a strip of wire.
> —Joyce Carol Oates, "The Hand-puppet"

Ghosts everywhere. Even the living were only ghosts in the
making. You learned to ration your commitment to them.
> —Pat Barker, *The Ghost Road*

Good old Banquo, atrocity's familiar, blood's henchman, unable
to die, but endowed with ghoulish adaptability, able to invade
and transcend any physique, state of mind, any afterlife even, in
the end destined by weird sisters or the power that told even
the Greek gods what to do, to perform an auto-da-fé on the last
human remaining.
> —Paul West, "Banquo and the Black Banana:
> The Fierceness of the Delight of the Horror"

GHOSTS AND DEATH

Certain events or cultural attitudes challenge the authority and enduring certainty of symbolic systems. As a historical event, the Holocaust
might be invoked. In literature, postmodernism comes to mind. According to Mark Taylor,

For the postmodern critic, modernity's dream of arrival is always a chimera. By returning us to a time "before the beginning," art and criticism remind us of what Mr. Blanchot describes as "the dreadfully ancient." Exceeding the alternative of presence and absence, this "dreadfully ancient" is the uncanny nothing that forever haunts the self-certain subject and deconstructs even our most valued constructions. For the listener who "beholds Nothing," experience is inevitably nomadic and thinking is inescapably unsettled and unsettling. Calling into question every certain conclusion, Mr. Derrida exposes the impossibility of all final solutions. ("Descartes, Nietzsche, and the Search for the Unsayable" 34. Originally published in *The New York Times,* February 1, 1987. Copyright © 1987 by The New York Times.)

Horror narrative has always treated experience in much the same terms, the ghost figure, in this context, being prototypal of the indeterminacy of signifiers. From some alternate landscape the apparition appears and everything changes; or, like Xavier Kilgarvan, we wander into some quicksand that relentlessly sucks away all human forms, including that of identity. These wanderings, in effect, bring us in destructive contact with mysterious, terrible forces, forces often given (or momentarily taking on) some hideous shape. Lovecraft spells out these contacts explicitly, but Oates also populates her Devil's Half-Acre with the ghost of a mad bishop, and even the narrator of Blackwood's "Willows" finds the bushes on the Danube beyond Vienna "forming a series of monstrous outlines" (Child, *Dark Company* 167). Actual history, of course, also has more than its share of monstrosities. Whatever explanations we try to bring to such phenomena (and, as I've noted, horror narratives from their confident critics to their desperate protagonists always attempt rational explanations), the final result must be always the same: a mere recognition of the movement from some kind of order to categorical disorder, nullity, chaos—an encounter, as Oates puts it so tellingly in *Mysteries of Winterthurn,* with "the greatest of Mysteries—to which there is no solution."

Obviously, the point here is the ubiquitous, overwhelming presence

and utter finality of death. Pat Barker, in one of her novels of the First
World War, reminds us that "even the living were only ghosts in the
making" (*Ghost Road* 46). In *The Cannibal* John Hawkes calls his prototypal German city Das Grab, the Tomb. Gerald Kennedy's treatment
of Poe's work focuses squarely on the centrality of death to it: as he
says, "not simply an isolated, unsolved problem in an essentially intel-
ligible world; it is the defining reality which enables one to see the
provisionality, even the unreality of our usual ways of conceptualizing
self and existence" (158).

Kennedy pursues the implications of this issue throughout Poe's
writing, but for our immediate purposes another of Oates's stories,
"Why Don't You Come Live With Me It's Time," sheds a direct, immediate light on the failure of the conceptualization invoked in
Kennedy. In this case as in so many others, the ghost is a mirror double
of any coherent, meaningful identity or any possible context in which
identity might be meaningful. In Oates's story, a young narrator called
Claire thinks her dead grandmother is staring at her, then realizes that
in fact she is staring at herself: "I saw the face was my own, my own
eyes in that face floating there not in a mirror but in a metallic mirrored surface, teeth bared in a startled smile" (Morrow & McGrath,
New Gothic 149). Like her grandmother, Claire is an insomniac, essentially a night dweller; when she does sleep, it is a fall into quicksand
("not water and not a transparency but an oozy lightless muck" [150]).
Waking is "to a sense of total helplessness and an exhaustion so profound it felt like death: sheer nonexistence, oblivion" (150). Like
Kennedy in his treatment of Poe, Oates makes clear that the issue with
both women is not so much psychological as metaphysical ("a malady
of the soul" [157]). A terrifying night visit to her beloved yet now dead
grandmother culminates for the narrator in a vision of the vulnerability of matter: "it came over me, the horror of it, that meat and bone
should define my presence in the universe: the point of entry in the
universe that was *me* that was *me* that was *me:* and no other: yet of a
fragile materiality that any fire could consume" (162).

Claire's awareness of her situation makes clear how explicitly she is, in effect, defining the essence of horror: matter unredeemed, matter consumed, without any dimension we might describe, at least in any positive sense, as human—certainly without any transcendental dimension. Indeed, Claire's first view of her grandmother/self in "a metallic mirrored surface" denies her even a significant subjectivity. Whatever its manifestations, the encounter with the ghost represents the intrusion of death in life, an intrusion suggesting not the transience of death but its ubiquitous and dominant presence in life as the "first principle" (the only principle?) of reality. Instead of life, in some fashion, extending beyond death, death, in fact, intrudes into life and destroys any meaning or value that we might bring to the act of living.

Another of Oates's stories uses the mirror image even more directly. In "The Temple" a fifty-year-old woman, who apparently has found some stability in her life, hears a "vexing, mysterious sound" in her garden and digs down among the "junglelike vegetation" and "shards of aged brick, glass, stones" to uncover finally a child's skull and some bones. Hamlet-like, "the woman lifted the skull to stare into the sockets as if staring into mirror-eyes, eyes of an eerie transparency" (*Collector of Hearts* 313–15). She lays out the remains on her bedside table and in effect turns her bedroom into a "secret temple" (316). Concerning the atavism here, the substantial intrusion of past into present, I have had a good deal to say already. Suffice it to note at this point that the mirror reveals the essential nature of our life and destiny.

In such contexts, the ghost or monster, a mirror of sorts, clearly represents a formal manifestation of one of the central themes of modernism, a theme heavily reinforced by much of the thrust of postmodernist criticism. In his important, far-ranging book *Rhetoric and Death* Ronald Schleifer describes his intentions as follows:

> I am trying to describe the modernist discovery of the material non-
> sense out of which signification is constructed in language and, analo-
> gous to this, a modernist recognition of death without transcendental

meaning, without signification beyond itself, simply, materially, and un-avoidably *there*. (9)

As he goes on to discuss at some length, modernism, on the whole, develops positive rhetorical responses to this always underlying and pervasive sense of death, while postmodernism brings rhetoric itself into question as a possible source of value. For our purposes, Schleifer's own use of language is revealing: he calls both modern art and life "haunted" by "a conception of life and meaning as fully and darkly arbitrary" (78), and he notes that "negativity haunts language like a ghost—the ghostliness of negative materiality" (211). Horror narrative, of course, makes explicit the ghost's presence in one form or another, and its implications are always categorically negative. In Paul West's appalling but vivid dramatic treatment, the voice of "good old Banquo" describes himself as "horror's ventriloquial doll" (Morrow & McGrath, *New Gothic* 58) and as "Lethe's proxy . . . a rentable death's-head doomed to float in and out of history" (55).

West's invocation of Banquo makes clear that ghosts are neither some recent invention of Western culture nor mere literary conventions, but he emphasizes also that, at least in later cultural contexts, they represent a growing failure of traditional signification, a failure that Kennedy, Schleifer, and many others make clear is felt with increasing acuteness. Michael Cox and R. A. Gilbert, the editors of *The Oxford Book of English Ghost Stories*, summarize a good deal of contemporary critical argument in suggesting that the nineteenth-and twentieth-century popularity of ghost stories represents both the deepening "malaise" of "theological doubt" and, ironically, some continuing commitment to "spiritualism." They add: "It may be that ghost stories, with their necessary insistence on the reality of life after death (however perverted and unfathomable), provided a buttress of sorts against materialism" (xiii).

Well, it may be; I leave such suppositions to others and stress only that the quality of life (assuming we are talking about life at all) has been drained of any positive dimension. Perhaps the question simply involves some degree of explicitness. Early in *Rhetoric and Death* Schleifer distinguishes between treating death as theme in narrative and his own concern with the concept of "negative materiality," which "traverses the discourse of modernism" and postmodernism and generates discourse, however vulnerable, "as a form of power and desire in modernist literature" (7–8). In this context, ghosts and other monsters represent death as explicit theme: antimatter made somehow visible or "palpable." After all, if horror is by definition the mystery of nothingness (or the metaphysics of nothingness), how *does* one make it palpable? The role and presence of the ghost is obviously central to the issue. Deconstructive parody, like a life-sucking parasite (the vampire image has perhaps more importance than we have recognized), complements or bonds with matter by way of "disembodying" it, by denying the sign its significance, where precisely the center of horror is the failure of the signifier. The ghost is the always accompanying Other; the issue is not (as usually thought) the locus of the ghost (i.e., internal projection or external manifestation) but its reality as the categorical presence of negation in the context of any positive affirmation.

In any case, central to horror narrative is the appearance of the negative double, and this appearance marks the end of positive possibilities. Ghosts, mysterious strangers, vampires, deviants, monsters, alien shapes—call them what you will—they are "shadows out of time" (to borrow the title of one of Lovecraft's more famous stories), and their arrival or manifestation changes everything. Like Oates's stories cited earlier, Jamaica Kincaid's "Ovando" is prototypal. The ghost arrives suddenly, mysteriously, arbitrarily:

A knock at the door.

It is Frey Nicolas de Ovando. I was surprised. I was not expecting him. But then on reflecting, I could see that though I was not expecting him, he was bound to come. Somebody was bound to come. On reflecting, I could see that while I sat I thought, Someone will come to

> me; if no one comes to me, then I will go to someone. There was that knock at the door. It was Ovando then. Immediately I was struck by his suffering. Not a shred of flesh was left on his bones; he was a complete skeleton except for his brain, which remained, and was growing smaller by the millennium. He stank. (Morrow & McGrath, *New Gothic* 3)

So Kincaid's story begins—with the entrance of a corpselike figure: "this stinky relic of a person" (3). He is horrible ("on a scale I did not even know existed before"), and he represents horror: "from his point of view he could see only horror and misery and disease and famine and poverty and nothingness" (5). He describes his arrival as "fated" and quickly settles into his "new home." But what is his old one like? From what alternate world does he come?

> Imagine whole countries populated by people with not a shred of flesh left on their bones, complete skeletons inside bodies made from plates of steel, people who had lost the ability to actually speak and could only make pronouncements, their brains growing smaller by the millennium, their bodies covered with blood in various shades of decay. (4)

A Satanic figure in a godless world, Ovando has prepared his own prophetic document, which includes the narrator:

> Then on this paper Ovando wrote that he dishonored me, that he had a right to do so for I came from nothing, that since I came from nothing I could not now exist in something, and so my existence was now rooted in nothing, and though I seemed to live and needed the things necessary to the living such as food and water and air, I was dead; and though I might seem present, in reality I was absent. This document consisted of hundreds of articles and each of them confirmed my dishonor, each of them confirmed my death, each of them confirmed my nothingness. (10)

From the teachings of her terrible visitor the narrator "exhausts" herself trying (probably futilely) to escape (13).

Obviously, Kincaid's story has political implications, even special meanings for her particular ethnic group. Similarly, from a Jewish perspective, Primo Levi describes his trip to Auschwitz as a "journey toward nothingness, a journey down there, toward the bottom" (13). Those surviving, however temporarily, "lay in a world of death and phantoms" (155). But the implications of any kind of horror narrative—phantomlike humanity in a universe of phantoms—go beyond the political just as they extend the meaning of what we might ordinarily call psychological. To be sure, ghosts are what the psychoanalyst and literary critic Julia Kristeva would call "abject figures." She describes the meanings of their corpselike presence as follows:

> In that compelling, raw, insolent thing in the morgue's full sunlight, in that thing that no longer matches and therefore no longer signifies anything, I behold the breaking down of a world that has erased its borders: fainting away. The corpse, seen without God and outside of science, is the utmost of abjection. It is death infecting life. Abject. It is something rejected from which one does not part, from which one does not protect oneself as from an object. Imaginary uncanniness and real threat, it beckons to us and ends up engulfing us. (*Powers of Horror* 4)

Horror narrative stresses the teleological implications of abjection; it is the ultimate literature of absence—from God, from substantial selfhood—and the ghost is its central character. It is no wonder that Mary Shelley in *Frankenstein* parodies *Paradise Lost;* horror narrative records loss, paradise gone and certainly not to be regained. Kristeva goes on to note that "all abjection is in fact recognition of the *want* on which any being, meaning, language, or desire is founded" (5). We are back to Taylor's gloss of Blanchot's "dreadfully ancient": "the uncanny nothing that forever haunts the self-certain subject and deconstructs even our most valued constructions" ("Descartes, Nietzsche" 34).

SOME GHOST STORIES:
THE SPECTRE REVEALED

In an excellent introduction to his collection of English ghost stories, Jack Sullivan notes that "the sense of lostness, of sudden helplessness in a malign universe, is the dominant theme in this fiction" (*Lost Souls* 8). He goes on to point out that "these stories are part of a modern experience depicted in literature in which absence is stronger, more powerfully infused with expectation, than anything present" (11). Particularly in translation, Kristeva's very language echoes with the imagery of ghosts. She speaks of one's being "haunted" by abjection, placed by it "literally beside himself" (or in French: "un pôle d'appel et de répulsion met celui qui en est habité littéralment hors de lui"), and elsewhere describes how "a massive and sudden emergence of uncanniness . . . now harries me as radically separate, loathsome. Not me. Not that. But not nothing, either. A 'something' that I do not recognize as a thing. A weight of meaninglessness, about which there is nothing insignificant, and which crushes me" (1, 2). The brilliant play of linguistic paradox here (nonentity that is "not nothing, either"; an unrecognizable "something"; significant meaninglessness (or in French: "Pas moi. Pas ça. Mais pas rien non plus. Un 'quelque chose' que je ne reconnais pas comme chose. Un poids de non-sens qui n'a rien d'insignifiant et qui m'écrase") precisely identifies the nature and meaning of the ghost figure.

Although obviously it may have psychological resonance, the significance of the double in horror narrative is not so much psychological as finally metaphysical, the principal convention of categorical inversion, the central manifestation of the dark side or view of things. The formless, menacing ghost of M. R. James's story "The Diary of Mr.

Poynter," for example, describes himself in his earlier life (he was the reprobate son of "an old worthy cavalier") as the Absalom who "believed he had shortened old David's days" (*Penguin Complete Ghost Stories* 233). Evil in horror narrative is simply the decreative force, substance, presence, or tendency—the Absalom in the life of every David—the crucial duality that threatens even the possibility of some sort of balanced alternative. Horror stories quite simply invite us—however confidently we may seem protected by whatever mantles of subjectivity we may have put on—to acknowledge and attempt to deal with this decreative Other.

With its relentless negative doubling, horror narrative endlessly replicates the Jekyll/Hyde situation, but before examining some of the more well known stories, let us look at a few examples of the form as a minor genre. We begin almost always with the impingement of that which comes from the alternate space described in Chapter 1. The catalytic event (like the knock on the door of Kincaid's Ovando) is the encounter with the demonic figure. Up "pops" this figure; the image of the Jack-in-the-box is explicitly used by M. R. James to suggest the imminent presence of lurking horror ("Residence at Whitminster," ibid. 224). As readers, according to the editors of *The Oxford Book of English Ghost Stories,* we become "anxious witnesses to a sudden and often fatal violation of everyday reality by the supernatural" (x).

Needless to say, our anxiety is nothing compared to the reactions of the principals in the various stories. Sheridan Le Fanu's "Schalken the Painter" is a case in point. Schalken, studying under the "immortal Gerald Douw," is in love with Douw's niece and wants to marry her, but one night a mysterious stranger appears and, in effect, buys the niece with rich gifts. His appearance enacts the experience of horror narrative—its arbitrariness, its brutal reversal of hope and love—and its description is worth full quotation:

These ardent labours, and worse still, the hopes that elevated and beguiled them [i.e., the plans of the lovers], were however, destined to ex-

perience a sudden interruption—of a character so strange and mysterious as to baffle all inquiry and to throw over the events themselves a
shadow of preternatural horror. (Sullivan, *Lost Souls* 17)

The young woman has apparently been won by a spectre (his face
"sensual, malignant, even satanic" [25]) and in due course becomes a
spectre herself. The story obviously mocks the pretensions of the immortal Douw: his moral callousness ("The record I have to make,"
writes the narrator, "is one of sordidness, levity, and heartlessness" [27])
and his vulnerability to ubiquitous death. Both spectres disappear, and
in the end we are left only with abiding mystery and uncertainty: "no
clue whereby to trace the intricacies of the labyrinth and to arrive at
its solution presented itself" (31). Horror narratives use much the same
material as the traditional mystery story, but their resolutions (or perhaps better to say, their failure of resolution) involve crucial differ-
ences. On this issue I will have much to say later. Here the painting
that Schalken later makes of the episode—a young and innocent
woman dressed in white and carrying a lamp menaced by the shadowy background figure of a man—represents (as the narrator says) "a
reality," but a reality without context or explanation (16).

In general, Le Fanu's nineteenth-century world is everywhere menacing and nowhere reassuring. Almost always the central encounter is
between a rational protagonist and some blocking force or figure—
something or someone radically other—that threatens the very prem-
ises of any rational order. "I shall sift this mystery to the bottom,"
thinks Sir Richard Marston in "The Evil Guest" (*Ghost Stories and
Mysteries* 252), when confronted by two mysterious visitors who seem
(he quickly comes to believe) to be plotting against him. He does not,
and is ruined in the trying; mysteries only deepen in the face of categorically new and dangerous contexts. To be sure, Le Fanu's doubling,
nominally at least, remains within the Christian context of heaven and
hell; his Satanic, demonic others generate at least the emotional energy
of pure and passionate malignity. In "The Mysterious Lodger," for ex-

ample, the lodger's explicit attack on what he calls "your Christian system" is delivered in a manner that "bespoke a sort of crouching and terrific hatred" (*Ghost Stories and Mysteries* 348). I am reminded of the description of the vampire Lestat in Anne Rice's "Freniere":

> Being a vampire for him meant revenge. Revenge against life itself. Every time he took a life it was revenge. It was no wonder, then, that he appreciated nothing. The nuances of vampire existence weren't even available to him because he was focused with a maniacal vengeance upon the mortal life he'd left. Consumed with hatred, he looked back. Consumed with envy, nothing pleased him unless he could take it from others; and once having it, he grew cold and dissatisfied, not loving the thing for itself; and so he went after something else. Vengeance, blind and sterile and contemptible. (*Morrow & McGrath, New Gothic* 80)

Rice's comment suggests a manifestation of essential negation (categorical nothingness, if you will) that goes well beyond the "Christian system"—indeed, beyond any system or possibility of system. The curious force or power of pure malignity remains as a presence destructive to all systems of whatever kind.

It is this power that Le Fanu expresses so well in his best-known story, "Green Tea." Here the apparition appears in the form of a grotesque black monkey and begins to haunt a scholarly clergyman. The narrator is one Dr. Martin Hesselius, whose perspective includes both that of the familiar nineteenth-century scientist/physician/detective (dedicated to the work of "analysis, diagnosis, and illustration" [Child, *Dark Company* 20]) and that of someone with metaphysical interests. In particular, Hesselius shares with the clergyman an interest in Swedenborg, an interest that, for the purposes of the story at least, involves a commitment to "evil spirits" ("the things that are in the other life" [27]). These spirits, under certain circumstances, become loose in our natural world. In this case, obviously, Swedenborg's theory of correspondences is used simply to rationalize a totally destructive duality. A powerful, malignant force of death intrudes on life ("to destroy any

man or spirit is the very delight of the life of all who are in hell" [27]),
and the clergyman finally commits suicide, though not before the
monkey has deconstructed all significant identity. At one point the
clergyman describes how the hypnotic monkey used to perch on fur-
niture and "slowly to swing itself from side to side, looking at me all
the time." And he adds:

> There is in its motion an indefinable power to dissipate thought, and to
> contract one's attention to that monotony, till the ideas shrink, as it
> were, to a point, and at last to nothing—and unless I had started up, and
> shook off the catalepsy I have felt as if my mind were on the point of
> losing itself. (40)

"Catalepsy" is the familiar stance of the haunted; here death merely
ratifies what the monkey all along has symbolized. "Dejected and agi-
tated," knowing the power of what he has witnessed ("It is the story of
the process of a poison" [46]), Dr. Hesselius nevertheless remains con-
vinced through the final pages that he might have saved his patient.
Toward this end he continues to offer us various pseudoscientific
"cures"—including, perhaps, even limitations on the drinking of
green tea. As a character type, he will reemerge more definitively in
the portrait of Dr. Van Helsing in *Dracula*. Incidentally, the tradition of
rationalist/scientist still goes on. Dr. John Montague, in Shirley Jackson's *Haunting of Hill House,* describes his "true vocation" (he has a degree in anthropology) as "the analysis of supernatural manifestations"
and self-consciously casts himself in the tradition of "the intrepid
nineteenth-century ghost hunters" (4).

Hesselius is scarcely convincing (his final remarks are addressed to
"those who suffer" [46]), even, I suspect, to himself. In horror literature the experience of catastrophe survives all explanations, including,
as I have noted, attempts by critics to complete at least the editorial
role failed by its protagonists. If such narrative is heavily formulaic, it is
nevertheless formula in the service of an intense theme that essentially

denies interpretation. The key episode is paradigmatic: first comes the encounter with a mysterious figure from obscure but deadly spaces; then the radical modifications of one's worldview (assuming survival at all) that such an encounter entails. I suspect equivalent experiences in real life follow a similar pattern: the deadly encounter; the radically changed point of view.

"There are powers of darkness which walk abroad in waste places: and that man is happy who has never had to face them" (Sullivan, *Lost Souls* 208). Such is the unequivocal theme of horror narrative and such, in one form or another, is what unsuspecting protagonists must deal with. In this case the quotation is from R. H. Malden's "Between Sunset and Moonrise," and reflects the sentiments of someone who survives a terrible encounter in the foggy English Fens. A scholarly and conscientious clergyman, he is returning one night along a narrow Fen road from a visit to the remote home of a parishioner when a "thick white mist" rolls up. Out of this mist comes the apparition:

> one solitary figure of gigantic stature rushing down the drove towards me at a fearful pace, without a sound. As he came the mist closed behind him, so that his dark figure was thrown up against a solid background of white: much as mountain climbers are said sometimes to see their own shadows upon a bank of cloud. On and on he came, until at last he towered above me and I saw his face. It has come to me once or twice since in troubled dreams, and may come again. But I am thankful that I have never had any clear picture of it in my waking moments. If I had I should be afraid for my reason. I know that the impression which it produced upon me was that of intense malignity long baffled, and now at last within reach of its desire. (206)

Perhaps I should have written that the clergyman *barely* survives; he suffers a nervous breakdown and never returns to his old parish. The parishioner herself is a curious figure. Described as witchlike in behavior and appearance, she has been reading the story of Sarah and the demon Asmodeus in the Book of Tobit and mysteriously dies that same night, perhaps after a visit from the fiend.

Aside from the baldness of its enactment of theme and its traditional invocation of what are here aptly called "waste places," Malden's story has two additional significant dimensions. One, doubling, involves usually not only some kind of matching with the ghost but also complementarity between the human protagonists, often one surviving while the other dies. Obviously, the catastrophic experience must reinforce the sense of death as malignant power in life; likewise, there must be some survivor to witness to an unbelieving world what has happened.

Equally significant in "Between Sunset and Moonrise" are the biblical references. Although Malden was writing during the atrocities of World War II, he chose rather to echo the long tradition of horror narrative by reminding us of a subculture of folklore and other apocryphal materials that have always suggested a darker view of life than modern religion and science normally emphasize, a view that war reinforces. With the heavy intervention of God, Asmodeus is finally routed in the Book of Tobit. In Malden's story, avoidance is our last (or should I say luckiest?) alternative. Of his own encounter, Malden's clergyman can only resort finally to the same metaphor of burial alive that Poe exploits so brilliantly: "there was the . . . feeling of pressure and suffocation . . . coupled with the most intense physical loathing. The only comparison which I can suggest is that I felt as a man might feel if he were buried under a heap of worms or toads" (206).

Burial alive, of course, is only the most literal version of a metaphor endemic to this kind of narrative: the underground passages, the terrible prisons, the hermetic rooms—all versions of living death, the active and central presence of death in life. To cite again the excellent writing of Gerald Kennedy on Poe:

[His] contemporaneity . . . comes from the perception of death as an absolute horizon of existence; . . . the essential horror of his writing resides in blankness and silence, in the perception of emptiness at the core of being. . . . His protagonists seem inescapably trapped by materiality, confined within coffins, vaults, dungeons, chambers, houses, and ships which are in some sense figures for the prison of corporality itself. (*Poe, Death* 211)

In a highly focused short story, "The Mine," L. T. C. Rolt describes (through a narrative voice) what he calls the "darkness being angry" of such places. They remind us at once of a past we may want to ignore—"they do say [the mine] was some old burial place when Adam was a boy-chap" (Sullivan, *Lost Souls* 325)—and a present that, as Kennedy suggests, may have established death as an absolute. From such darknesses emerges the ghost, the prototypical figure of darkness. In Rolt's story (and again in narrative dialect) "it had a human shape . . . even if it did seem terrible tall and thin, and it seemed to be a kind of dirty white all over, like summat that's grown up in the dark, and never had no light" (329). Here the traditional white of ghosts is "dirty" enough to suggest the profound, indeed categorical, soiling of darkness.

War, naturally, can only enhance a sense of deadly doubling. The Other represents perhaps an alter ego who does not escape death, perhaps a terrible enemy counterpart who actively seeks one's murder. In any case, the menacing spook is always a threat. I have already noted that, for American troops, the Vietnamese landscape was haunted by spooks. "The Travelling Grave" by L. P. Hartley explicitly invokes the context of World War I. The protagonist, Hugh Curtis, has always had a vivid sense of living in a "killing" world, a sense that the war has only confirmed. He heads for a weekend at an English country estate (a new killing ground, as these splendid estates so often are in horror narratives) and barely escapes death from a mechanical coffin, which destroys relentlessly and at random ("it seemed to have no settled direction, and to move all ways at once, like a crab" [Sullivan, *Lost Souls*

116]). Jack Sullivan's editorial comment here makes the crucial point: "Hugh finds himself in an absurd postwar world where they are still trying to kill him" (109). Pat Barker often invokes ghosts and has aptly titled the third volume of her World War I trilogy *The Ghost Road*. The twentieth century seemed endlessly to be either at war or postwar. "The Scar," by Ramsey Campbell, relates the encounter of the protagonist with a savage doppelgänger ("the idea being that if you saw your double it meant you were going to die" [Sullivan, *Lost Souls* 396]), a figure associated with the bombing of Liverpool: "Was this the key? Had someone been driven underground by blitz conditions, or had something been released by bombing? In either case, what form of camouflage would they have had to adopt to live?" (408). As usual, the "key" remains mysterious, but the horror nevertheless spreads relentlessly and ubiquitously over the events of the story.

I have already noted that it is scarcely possible (and perhaps even positively misleading) to separate out editorially Ambrose Bierce's war stories from those of horror. In his well-known "Chickamauga," for example, the figures on the battlefield are men in the morning, maimed, animalic shapes by nightfall, dragging themselves along "like a swarm of great black beetles" (*Complete Short Stories* 316). Bierce's imagery everywhere reinforces the implications of these debased figures: the "horrible comparisons" (of the naive little boy observer), their "ghastly gravity," the "haunted landscape" through which they move and cast their "monstrous shadows" (316). All this horror, incidentally, is at least implicitly atavistic; it is set against the little boy's heroic dreams, more generally against the entire program of Western culture, "trained to memorable feats of discovery and conquest" (313).

A "civil" war, of course, almost by definition involves relentless doubling of one kind or another. Bierce's "Mocking-Bird" literally enacts fratricide: a Union soldier on sentinel duty kills a shadowy intruder, only to discover later that he has shot a beloved twin brother separated from him early in life and raised as a southerner. Probably most significant for Bierce are the deconstructive implications of war—undoubtedly those implications that generate the appearance of ghosts. He describes night sentry duty, for example, as involving a radical challenge to perception:

> But all was now different; he saw nothing in detail, but only groups of things, whose shapes, not observed when there was something more of them to observe, were now unfamiliar. They seemed not to have been there before. A landscape that is all trees and undergrowth, moreover, lacks definition, is confused and without accentuated points upon which attention can gain a foothold. Add the gloom of a moonless night, and something more than great natural intelligence and a city education is required to preserve one's knowledge of direction. (364)

It is under such circumstances that Private Grayrock "lost his bearings" and encountered a ghost.

Obviously, for Bierce war early on subverted the law of probabilities on which literary realism depends and which horror narrative denies. In a more conventional ghost story, "The Secret of Macarger's Gulch," the narrator finds himself in a remote house in a remote place as night comes on. He fears the darkness within as much as that without; both challenge whatever comforts the law of probabilities might seem to offer. Seated inside before a small hearth, he notes:

> I was unable to repress a certain feeling of apprehension as my fancy pictured the outer world and filled it with unfriendly entities, natural and supernatural—chief among which, in their respective classes, were the grizzly bear, which I knew was occasionally still seen in that region, and the ghost, which I had reason to think was not. Unfortunately, our feelings do not always respect the law of probabilities, and to me that evening, the possible and the impossible were equally disquieting. (*Complete Short Stories* 33)

In this "disquieting" world, the darkness finally becomes "absolute," and the violence associated with the house is reenacted—a reenactment that gives such violence (or violence in general) the status of a permanent condition. As Bierce puts it in another story: "In the spiritual, as in the material world, are signs and presages of night" (*Complete Short Stories* 39). What they presage is death, and, for Bierce at least, "in the presence of death reason and philosophy are silent" (88).

Bierce's stories enact what they have forecast, and what they forecast is categorically inimical to life, hope, and happiness. Their central parable rehearses the "seeming suspension," failure, or total loss of significant forms, what he describes as "the orderly operation of familiar natural laws" (101)—obviously a wartime scenario that can easily have more sweeping implications. In Bierce's stories the ghosts are essentially those of figures who witness (affirm and represent) an alternate world, both that Realm of Terror beyond the grave and that presumably familiar place where we attempt to live out our lives. These negative doubles represent a radical change in perspective; they widen our sense of reality but at the expense of emphasizing what Bierce calls its "perils." In "The Moonlit Road" the ghost describes her point of view (through a medium) as follows:

> You think that we are of another world. No, we have knowledge of no world but yours, though for us it holds no sunlight, no warmth, no music, no laughter, no song of birds, nor any companionship. O God! what a thing it is to be a ghost, cowering and shivering in an altered world, a prey to apprehension and despair! (142)

In Bierce's fiction it is precisely this "altered world" that intrudes so horribly on our own.

Such an intrusion is central to *The Turn of the Screw*, probably the horror narrative most well known and certainly the one that has generated the widest variety of interpretations. We return—as Joyce would say by "a commodious vicus of recirculation"—to James's great story, now more securely able to place it in a long and significant tradition of narrative. Obviously, certain other critics are aware of some

of the conditions of horror narrative. I have already noted, for example, Joyce Carol Oates's version of life for the ghosts beyond the
grave and Shoshana Felman's argument regarding the impossibility of
explanatory interpretation. Let me, with James's help, simply spell out
a few implications a bit more. James is, as usual, his own best critic,
someone with a sophisticated awareness of the tradition he so powerfully invokes. For Bierce, in an effective ghost story "you must be
made to feel fear—at least a strong sense of the supernatural—and that
is a difficult matter" (*Complete Short Stories* 224). James could not agree
more, but he is able (critically and creatively) to develop such a thesis
much further. This development is in directions I have already empha-
sized: toward the fundamental thematic implications of horror narrative, toward the role of the ghosts, and toward certain stylistic issues,
particularly the use of narrator, which I will deal with at some length
in Chapter 3.

In the preface to the New York Edition, James calls *The Turn of the
Screw* "an excursion into chaos" (Norton Critical Edition 120)—a
statement that stands not only as an apt description of his story but,
more generally, as the most useful brief definition of the function and
theme of horror narrative that we are ever likely to have. His statement cuts in at least two directions, both relevant to our discussion.
On the one hand, it emphasizes the radical indeterminacy of his own
and all horror narrative, which everywhere embraces mystery over
causal statements that might reduce, locate, or otherwise explain it
away. Horror narrative merely invites us to witness certain events. The
narrator at the beginning of H. P. Lovecraft's "The Tomb" states
bluntly: "It is sufficient for me to relate events without analysing
causes" (*Tomb and Other Tales* 7). Such statements are ubiquitous in the
form. At issue for James is simply the control of tone: "of suspected
and felt troubles, of an inordinate and incalculable sore—the tone of
tragic, yet exquisite mystification" (120). As the author, he was to
"knead the subject of my young friend's, the supposititious narrator's,
mystification thick, and yet strain the expression of it so clear and fine

that beauty would result" (120). He goes on to describe what he calls
the governess's labyrinthine experiences ("my young woman engaged
in her labyrinth" [120]) and makes, finally, the crucial distinction between recording and explanation. It was of central importance to him,
"the general proposition of our young woman's keeping crystalline
her record of so many intense anomalies and obscurities—by which I
don't of course mean her explanation of them, a different matter"
(121). In James's version, at least, chaos is not subject to any formula-
tion except, paradoxically, the aesthetic organization that gives it expression in the first place (the resulting "beauty").

On the other hand, chaos and mystery have sharper, more explicit
moral and metaphysical implications than I have so far suggested; and
in his commentaries, at least, James nowhere seems to shy away from
these implications. He makes clear, for example, in his preface, that the
function of his story was "to rouse the dear old sacred terror," that his
aim was *not* to write a "new type . . . the mere modern 'psychical' case
washed clean of all queerness" (118). This last statement is particularly
ironic in the light of all the psychological explanations that have attempted to cleanse the work. He tells us slightly further on that, in as-
sembling his materials, he was "to remember the haunted children and
the prowling servile spirits as a 'value,' of the disquieting sort, in all
conscience sufficient" (118). He describes *The Turn of the Screw* as a
"sinister romance" (118). An early notebook entry summarizes a possible plot: "The servants, wicked and depraved, corrupt and deprave
the children; the children are bad, full of evil, to a sinister degree"
(106). Later, to someone who has read the story and is apparently
puzzled by it he writes:

> The thing that, as I recall it, I most wanted not to fail of doing, under
> penalty of extreme platitude, was to give the impression of the commu-
> nication to the children of the most infernal imaginable evil and dan-
> ger—the condition, on their part, of being as *exposed* as we can humanly
> conceive children to be. This was my artistic knot to untie. (112)

To be sure, James, in the same letter, speaks of *The Turn of the Screw* as "an inferior, a merely *pictorial,* subject and rather a shameless pot-boiler" (112); but this comment (aside from its being an attempt to avoid pretentiousness) probably reflects his awareness of the narrowness of horror narrative, particularly given its easy and frequent vulgarization in popular literature—what James acknowledges as a "pot-boiler" dimension.

In fact, James perfectly understands the power and significance of narrowness. However limited horror narrative may seem as a comprehensive and varied expression of the possibilities of life and death, it is, nevertheless, unflinching as a categorical expression of negation both material and metaphysical. God, says David Grossvogel in his excellent book *Mystery and Its Fictions,* represents "man's most strenuous effort to overcome mystery," and he goes on to note the "sense of darkness and danger that lurks on the other side of understanding" (5). In *The Turn of the Screw* God is either absent or nonexistent (like the bachelor guardian of the children, who wants "never, never" to be troubled by them [6]), but this does not for a minute suggest to James the possibility of an alternate secular order. Rather, his nineteenth-century mind shares acutely in the "sense of darkness and danger" mentioned by Grossvogel. As early as 1865 he noted that Wilkie Collins had brought horror narrative up to date: from Radcliffe's Apennine castles we had moved "to the terrors of the cheerful country-house and the busy London lodgings." Amid "the common objects of life" had emerged, with renewed credibility, awareness of "the numberless possible forms of human malignity" (97–98). A few years before *The Turn of the Screw,* Melville in *Billy Budd* was also trying to bring Radcliffe up to date; he located a "mysterious" depravity in Claggart and then groped for a definition that conveyed a power both relentless and categorical.

In any case, the issue for James involves a world "of the most infernal imaginable evil and danger"—a world all the more evil and dangerous because iniquity is without definite location and cause, everywhere and specifically nowhere. As the wide range of criticism directed to the story might suggest, *The Turn of the Screw* deconstructs almost every material and transcendental myth cherished by the nineteenth century: the innocence of childhood, the benign ("cheerful" in James's words) English country house with its magic gardens, the loving, angelic, protective mother, the overarching patriarchal presence, symbolic of control and order, and doubtless many others. The governess's background in a rural parsonage and her faith in its conventional pieties (in her ordeal involving something "revoltingly against nature" she will bring "only another turn of the screw of ordinary human virtue" [80]) are probably as significant as Lord Jim's similar origins in Conrad's novel of two years later. Both books announce a twentieth-century world cut loose, like Jim and the governess, from the comfortable values of nineteenth-century Western culture to wander in a chaotic universe.

Concerning the function of the ghosts in horror narrative—his own and those generic to the form—James has equal insight. They are, of course, negative doubles of the central masculine and feminine roles of the novella. Joyce Carol Oates, as I have already noted, describes explicitly the underground "night" world where they now dwell and from which they emerge to act out (or reenact) a terrible drama of uncontrolled, endlessly unsatisfied, perverse and savage desire, or, as Oates puts it, "desire without consummation" (*Haunted* 265).

James, rather, invokes the world of dark and dangerous fairyland so characteristic of the nineteenth-century ghost story and, uncharacteristically, writes a romance ("I cast my lot with pure romance" [121]). In this context, he goes on to say:

> I recognize again, that Peter Quint and Miss Jessel are not "ghosts" at all, as we know the ghost, but goblins, elves, imps, demons as loosely constructed as those of the old trials for witchcraft; if not, more pleasingly, fairies of the legendary order, wooing their victims forth to see them dance under the moon. (122)

Not, that is, modern "psychical" ghosts (as he calls them), but certainly not some kind of "pleasing" fairies either. "The essence of the matter," James explains,

> was the villainy of motive in the evoked predatory creatures; so that the result would be ignoble—by which I mean would be trivial—were this element of evil but feebly or inanely suggested. Thus arose on behalf of my idea . . . the question of how best to convey that sense of the depths of the sinister without which my fable would so woefully limp. Portentous evil—how was I to save that, as an intention on the part of my demon-spirits, from the drop, the comparative vulgarity, inevitably attending, throughout the whole range of possible brief illustration, the offered example, the imputed vice, the cited act, the limited deplorable presentable instance? (122)

"Portentous evil" (presumably something both prophetic and extraordinary): that is the "essence" of his fable and that is the essence of horror narrative in general. "The haunting pair," he adds, are capable "of everything" (122). At least potentially, horror is ubiquitous, subject only to the limits of our "appreciation, speculation, imagination" (122). Certainly any positive value system that might finally point toward expiation is out of the question: "There is not only from beginning to end of the matter not an inch of expiation, but my values are positively all blanks save so far as an excited horror, a promoted pity, a created expertness . . . proceed to read into them more or less fantastic figures" (123). As Shoshana Felman has noted, the governess, like her many critics, tries to play detective and solve the mystery but finally grasps only death. According to Felman, "the very enterprise of appropriating meaning is thus revealed to be the strict appropriation of precisely *nothing*—nothing alive at least" (*Writing and Madness* 216). Oates describe her ghosts as "insufficiently dead" (*Haunted* 265). Her apt phrase probably suggests that the demonism so often associated with horror narrative—which might involve a Satanic universe cen-

tered on evil—rather expresses a sense of incompletion, fragmenta-
tion, unfulfillment, unrequited desire, savage neediness in an endless
and hopeless quest for order, not really centeredness of any kind so
much as absence of every kind.

Monstrosity within and without, monstrosity everywhere, that is
what James suggests and horror narrative everywhere affirms. In "The
Jolly Corner," his other great ghost story, James invites us from the
very beginning to identify the ghost as some monstrous alter ego—
some terrible Other—something "quite hideous and offensive," according to his protagonist, Spencer Brydon (Child, *Dark Company* 58).
Whereas in *The Turn of the Screw* the governess tries reactively to deal
with the ghosts from some dark alternative space who presumably
have invaded and now inhabit her comfortable and conventional English rural world, Brydon obsessively (releasing his "stifled perversity"
[59]) seeks out this dark space and increasingly finds it more meaningful than his daytime world or even the ordinary night world beyond
the (usually closed) windows of his empty and abandoned house. Brydon's quest into "this mystical other world" (62) becomes essentially, as
James is well aware, a parody of the traditional knightly quest for spiritual vision. The narrative voice (here, at least, close to the perspective
of Brydon himself) makes this specific point: "what age of romance,
after all, could have matched either the state of his mind, or 'objec-
tively,' as they said, the wonder of the situation?" (67). Brydon notes
elsewhere that "he had been surprised at any rate—of this he was
aware—into something unprecedented" (66).

Certainly he finds wonders of a sort; clearly they are, in their own
way, unprecedented. I am reminded of the title of Aharon Appelfeld's
novel *The Age of Wonders,* a work dealing with upper-middle-class Jews
in Austria just before World War II, moving inexorably from uneasy as-
similation toward the Holocaust. In any case, the crucial action of
James's story involves Brydon's turning from an ordinary reality
("human actual social; this was . . . the world he had lived in" [63]) to
an alternate extraordinary one. Previously he has found such ordinary

reality incalculable (the great fact . . . had been the uncalculability" [50]), and his return to America only reinforces this feeling. Now, relentlessly pursuing some higher vision, Brydon enters his shuttered house and into a labyrinthine world of horrors—a Gothic (or, as we might say today, a Kafkaesque) universe of endless corridors, staircases, opening and shutting doors (with their persistent hint of some symbolic threshold to be crossed)—and at last barely escapes death, the horrible "black stranger" (79) waiting at the end. Whomsoever or whatever the stranger may finally represent, his downcast face and mutilated hand suggest at least the nature and cost, indeed imminent danger, of this alternative space and its ghostly inhabitants.

MORE SUBSTANTIAL MONSTERS

We have talked about nothing but monsters in this chapter and can only continue to do so. Conventionally, ghosts, of course, resemble the living human beings they once were, but often they come forward as horribly misshapen, sometimes even taking bizarre animal forms. The figure that Brydon encounters in "The Jolly Corner" has two missing fingers. In Arthur Machen's "Great God Pan" a doomed woman retains a changing female shape after her terrible initiation into the spirit of Pan. The disgusting figure unearthed in Walter de la Mare's "A : B : O" is more obviously and explicitly a hideous human travesty. And finally—to round out our almost random list of ghostly avatars— the negative force in Le Fanu's "Green Tea" expresses itself as a monkey.

But horror narrative, as I am defining it, has a wider basis in literature and life than the so-called ghost story, and its monsters (Mr. Hyde, Dracula, and Frankenstein's monster, to note a few obvious examples, not to mention such figures as Maturin's Melmoth and "Monk" Lewis's Ambrosio from an earlier period and the endless angels of death who populate actual history) are, in general, more substantial, complex, and highly developed than anything I have so far suggested. To be sure, their role as negative extension or double of the protagonist remains—a doubling central and obvious in Stevenson's *Dr. Jekyll and Mr. Hyde* and one we have already noted in Lovecraft's "Shadow Out of Time," where avatars of the Great Race ("monstrous objects") express themselves through contemporary human beings. Such a takeover by alien figures remains a principal motif of horror narrative in its role as a staple of popular culture. H. G. Wells was another influential creator of these "Other-Worlds" (as he called them), whether they existed already peopled as some kind of fourth dimension or because of human acts of atrocity—Dr. Moreau reenacting the earlier role of Frankenstein.

In any case, literary monsters at least, over some extended period of time, become what Saul Bellow's Herzog (recollecting the function of some of his acquaintances) calls our "reality-instructors," directly and indirectly teaching us not only about ourselves but about the larger cosmos extending beyond any possible extension of personal identity. Terms conventionally used to label monsters—deviants, grotesques, madmen, demons, misanthropes, misfits, malign parodies, negative identities—are useful insofar as they describe the decentered and de-centering role of the monsters, less useful if they imply that such de-centering can be dealt with by various kinds of social engineering. Judith Halberstam, for example, in *Skin Shows* splendidly defines monstrosity as "embodied horror" (2–3) but then focuses on a recent historical context:

> the emergence of the monster within Gothic fiction marks a peculiarly modern emphasis upon the horror of particular kinds of bodies. Furthermore, the ability of the Gothic story to take the imprint of any number of interpretations makes it a hideous offspring of capitalism itself. The Gothic novel of the nineteenth century and the Gothic horror film of the late twentieth century are both obsessed with multiple modes of consumption and production, with dangerous consumptions and excessive productivity, and with economies of meaning. The monster itself is an economic form in that it condenses various racial and sexual threats to nation, capitalism, and the bourgeoisie in one body. (3)

Contexts, of course, are important and contain their own significance, but they can be misleading. The implications in the passage above of a need for change are obvious; as Halberstam later writes concerning film Gothic: "feminist and queer responses to these Gothic modalities are most certainly called for if we are to make a claim for the positivity of horror" (26). In other words, with a change in cultural attitudes—or at least some appropriate political actions—we might be able to take a positive view of horror as potentially ameliorative. Horror might not be so horrible after all!

But I am scarcely being fair to Halberstam. I simply cite her book, which, in general, has many useful things to say about horror, to mark a tendency of recent criticism. From my perspective, on the contrary, horror narrative in its monsters, as well as in all its other dimensions, registers a permanent condition, not only of the self but of any higher reality in which we may choose to include ourselves. As Oates puts it: "the grotesque always possesses a blunt *physicality* that no amount of epistemological exegesis can exorcise" (*Haunted* 304). Indeed, far from suggesting the possibility of some kind of personal or social amelioration, monstrous creatures may even have the opposite effect on us. Oates goes on to note that "this is the forbidden truth, the unspeakable taboo—that evil is not always repellent but frequently attractive; that it has the power to make of us not simply victims, as nature and accident do, but active accomplices" (305–6). In this context, two figures not perhaps obviously identified as monsters—Bonaventura's night watchman and Maturin's Melmoth—offer significant models.

Die Nachtwachen des Bonaventura (The Night Watches of Bonaventura, 1804–5) is a curious book. Its author is unknown (Bonaventura being a pseudonym), and it is divided into sixteen episodic "night watches," each of which explodes some dimension of European high romanticism, as the narrative voice (Kreuzgang, the night watchman) mocks the pretensions of those he encounters in his wanderings. In these encounters with various manifestations of a movement that, in the West at least, represents the last substantial attempt to imagine a universe both human and God-centered, the voice is categorically

negative, comprehensive, totally decentering. As the editor and transla-
tor Gerard Gillespie points out (quoting from the earlier criticism of
Jeffrey Sammons), the episodes insofar as they have structure bore
"ever deeper into the empty core of the universe" (2). Gillespie goes
on to note that this process is relentlessly and categorically entropic:
"Everything, both biological entities and art are perceived to be returning to the realm of lifelessness, dis-organization" (22). And he
notes also the final implications of this movement:

> The trend is toward perversion and even annihilation—all creation is
> tragic through its own inherent principle. The idea of entropy seems to
> imply the correlative of suicide for the identity within its universe. In
> this sense, the final cry of the book is simultaneously a moment when
> Nothingness overwhelms Kreuzgang and when his mind merges with
> the universal process and end of being. (16)

Whatever cross he may bear, the narrator functions only as a dark parody of possibility, and the last word of the book is indeed "NOTH-
ING"—a theme, here explicitly articulated, that links horror narrative
to an important dimension of modernism.

As monster, Kreuzgang remains ghostlike, an endless hovering presence, but now one on a scale of magnitude and complexity that seeks
to encompass all experience. His stance invokes the total inversion of
all positive perspectives; as he observes with bitter wit: "either people
are standing on their heads or I am" (113). For Kreuzgang, death is
ubiquitous, the only reality, and he will be its spokesperson. As he argues vividly and powerfully:

> The death's-head is never missing behind the ogling mask and life is
> only the cap and bells which the Nothing has draped around to tinkle
> with and finally to tear up fiercely and hurl from itself. Everything is
> Nothing and vomits itself up and gulps itself greedily down, and even
> this self-devouring is an insidious sham, as if there were something
> whereas, if the choking were once to cease, precisely the Nothing

would quite plainly make its appearance and all would be terrorstruck before it; by this cessation, fools understand "eternity"; but it is the real Nothing and absolute death, since life, on the contrary, only arises through a continual dying. (141)

Kreuzgang's point of view obviously mocks the Christian implications of his name and even denies any redemptive possibilities to classical tragedy. He will, he says, limit the action of tragedy "as much as possible, so that man, that Oedipus, progress only as far as blindness, but not in a second plot to transformation" (142–43). In his unwavering commitment to irrationality, Kreuzgang is mad, to be sure, but he acknowledges, even celebrates his madness, associating himself with such prototypical "blasphemers" as Satan and the Wandering Jew, all those who insist on articulating only suffering and death in a counterpart universe of horror.

While in the madhouse himself, Kreuzgang fantasizes "the establishment of a fools' propaganda and propagation of an expanded colony of crazies, in order to have them suddenly disembark to the terror of the other rational men" (201)—a fantasy, incidentally, literally enacted in *The Cannibal,* John Hawkes's important narrative dealing with the horrors of modern Germany. One scene of Hawkes's book describes how the "devouring" inhabitants of an insane asylum are set free to add their weight to an already cannibalistic community. On this particular issue, Kreuzgang has, as always, his own bitterly ironic view: "man is a devouring creature, and if one only throws a lot to him, then in the hours of digestion the most splendid things issue from him and he is transfigured eating and becomes immortal" (185). The night watchman's vivid wit belies the utterly focused and committed seriousness of his author. As Peter Thorslev has noted in his valuable attempt to sort out the complexities of romanticism, "the Gothic poet [against all our worldly and transcendental forms of hope] asserts the intuition that there is no universal order, rational or moral" (*Romantic Contraries* 131). In other words, the propagation of crazies will at least destroy deceptive and absurd illusions. This passion for reality links horror narrative in its various manifestations with all serious art and gives it more dignity and significance than many contextualizing critical explanations might suggest.

With Kreuzgang it is essentially his ironic voice that is deconstructive. Most monsters, while embodying and even articulating negation, play a more active role in bringing it about. They enact what they everywhere manifest and affirm. Maturin's Melmoth is a case in point, though even Melmoth (with traditional Catholic symbolism still clinging to him and the world he inhabits) lacks the concreteness and specificity of the more naturalistic nineteenth-century generations, not to mention actual historical figures. In any case, Maturin, like the earlier pseudonymous Bonaventura, widens the scope of horror narrative and in so doing immeasurably heightens its significance and marks the road to come. Automatism, endless sterile repetition that lacks positive closure, gives nullity in Bonaventura's *Night Watches* and other horror narratives a strong metaphysical extension. Even irony, as Judith Wilt has noted, may be included, "the fear that even 'that ghastly and derisive smile' of self-mockery many now be simply automatic" (*Ghosts of the Gothic* 60). Kreuzgang makes the same point about his own attitudes. Wilt also reminds us of Milton's "unholy" creation of Satan, Sin, and Death. We have encountered this last figure before, and Wilt goes on to give it telling definition: "Death, the final inevitable term in the series of Satan's being, the Unholy Ghost, spirit of decreation emerges . . . to breathe upon the new earth his invitation to return to eldest night and chaos, where all movement is either purposeless strife or blind rigidity" (68).

Paradise Lost has at least its double trinities; horror narrative has only its unholy ghosts. Such a drastic narrowing of focus exposes the central paradox of horror narrative: its insistence (indeed, more vehemently and self-consciously than most narrative forms) on a dualism that some endlessly repeated action everywhere collapses. In his "Full Statement" Henry Jekyll acknowledges his early commitment "to a profound duplicity of life" and later begins to realize "that man is not truly one, but truly two" (*Dr. Jekyll and Mr. Hyde* 78–79). In fact, Jekyll/Hyde increasingly becomes only Hyde, a figure given over totally to horror and death. Jekyll attempts to disavow his double ("He, I say—I cannot say, I. That child of Hell had nothing human; nothing lived in him but fear and hatred" [98]), but finally makes clear that dualism has collapsed. When he wakes from even a brief doze, he admits, "it was always as Hyde that I awakened" (100). Horror narrative involves us with mordant attitudes and parodic structures that invoke dualism without really preserving it (albeit in some attenuated form) but rather destroys all positive possibilities while endlessly and painfully reminding us of the forms of hope.

Certainly, Melmoth acts "always as Hyde," Antichrist without his positive counterpart, a figure of death and nullity beyond the grave ("superhuman misanthropy," in Maturin's term [233]), who mirrors and actively invokes these qualities in actual life (affirming only "a world of suffering, guilt, and care" [218]), the incarnation of everyone's most extreme despair—its symbolic center, recorder, spokesperson. Nominally the traditional tempter (an end to suffering, if you will abandon hope of heaven), Melmoth is more fundamentally an ironic voice that deconstructs all hope ("a spirit that mingled ridicule with horror, and seemed like a Harlequin in the infernal regions, flirting with the furies" [390]). His traditional Satanic role merely reflects the implications of his larger performances. Maturin describes him as "one who had traversed life from Dan to Beersheba, and found all barren, or made it so" (391).

Maturin's word "traversed" has implications that go beyond the obvious. To be sure, *Melmoth the Wanderer* is a compendium of Gothic motifs that stretch from Walpole to Poe and beyond: the convent world of closed rooms, high walls, hermetic entrapment; the tortuous and labyrinthine passages turning back on themselves; the torments of the Inquisition; the endless brutal and arbitrary "fathers." All this, of course, reflects the traditional prejudices of a Protestant culture, and the harsh male figures additionally have implications for feminist criticism. In earlier horror narrative, Catholicism becomes a distancing (and thus available and potent) metaphor of negative metaphysical ideas associated with whatever malignant superior or director heads the religious order in question. Imaginative distancing, incidentally, allows Maturin to have it both ways politically; by 1820 conventions can be both freely invoked and self-consciously played against. Through one of his endless narrative voices he tells us to "expect no romance-horrors" from his narrative. Rather, he will present us with "facts instead of images" (168). On another occasion, Maturin even more emphatically disassociates his work from romance:

> Romances have been written and read, whose interest arose from the noble and impossible defiance of the heroine to all powers human and superhuman alike. But neither the writers or readers seem ever to have taken into account the thousand petty external causes that operate on human agency with a force, if not more powerful, far more effective than the grand internal motive which makes so grand a figure in romance, and so rare and trivial a one in common life. (285)

The context here involves one of his own heroines, trapped, as usual, by a "thousand petty external causes" that defeat her. Yet these same conventions allow Maturin technically to distance himself from his own savage misanthropy. On one rare occasion, a footnote warns us to preserve a distance between narrator and author: "I must here trespass so far on the patience of the reader as to assure him, that the sentiments ascribed to the stranger are diametrically opposite to mine, and that I have purposely put them into the mouth of an agent of the enemy of mankind" (233). Perhaps, after all, Maturin, like Henry James, is simply writing "a shameless pot-boiler."

But one suspects more, a lot more. Melmoth is as much a ghost as any I have described, and his negations "traverse" all our attempts at creative structuring. Of her illegal marriage to Melmoth, Isidora re-